PAINLESS
Speaking

Mary Elizabeth, M.Ed.

illustrated by Denise Gilgannon

BARRON'S

All inquiries should be addressed to:
Barron's Educational Series, Inc.
250 Wireless Boulevard
Hauppauge, New York 11788
http://www.barronseduc.com

Library of Congress Catalog Card No.: 2002074489

ISBN-13: 978-0-7641-2147-0
ISBN-10: 0-7641-2147-2

Library of Congress Cataloging-in-Publication Data

Mary Elizabeth (Mary Elizabeth Podhaizer)
    Painless speaking / Mary Elizabeth.
        p.   cm.
        Summary: Discusses oral communication from uttering a sound,
    effects of culture, conversational speech, reading alone or with
    others, prepared speaking and speaking with little or no preparation,
    and more.
        ISBN 0-7641-2147-2
        1. Oral communication–Juvenile literature. [1. Oral
    communication. 2. Speech. 3. Public speaking.] I. Title.
    P95 .M333 2002
    302.242–dc21

                                                    2002074489

PRINTED IN CANADA

9 8 7 6 5 4

To John H. Clarke,
who was there when some ideas began to grow
and who helped them on their way
—with my gratitude

Acknowledgments

Appreciation goes to readers who commented on the manuscript, including Robert Hoberman, Marc Hull, Bernier Mayo, and Michael Podhaizer. Thanks to my Barron's editor, Linda Turner, and to Ann Laberge and Dr. John Bisaccia for permission to use their writings. Special thanks to Xan Johnson for permission to use the scene from his play and for his assistance with preparation of sections of the manuscript related to his specialty of youth theatre.

The author gratefully acknowledges the following copyright holders for permission to reprint their work.

Pages 45–48: Diagrams 1–5, the original diagram and its adaptations—*Diagram: The Intentional Relation of Identity* from "Semiotic and a Theory of Knowledge" from THE MESSAGE IN THE BOTTLE by Walker Percy. Copyright © 1975 by Walker Percy. Reprinted by permission of Farrar, Straus and Giroux, LLC.

Page 101: Program Cover: *The New Survivors: A Collage of Images from the Holocaust*, designed by Jann Haworth, Copyright © 2002. [Jann Haworth was awarded a Grammy as the Co-designer of the Beatles' *Sgt. Pepper* cover. She was Visual Arts Director at Sundance Artisan Center in Sundance, Utah (tutor in fine art painting, drawing, and sculpture).]

Pages 273–276: "Golf Fitness: What You Don't Know Might Hurt You" by Dr. John J. Bisaccia, Certified Sports Chiropractic Physician, Copyright © 2002.

Pages 277–279: "NELL'S KITTENS: An Analogy" by A. D. Laberge, Copyright © 2002.

Pages 280–286: A scored cutting taken from the script *The New Survivors: A Collage of Images from the Holocaust, Scene Two: Terezin—We Must Survive!* By Xan S. Johnson, Ph.D., Young Peoples' Theatre Specialist, University of Utah, Copyright © 2002.

CONTENTS

INTRODUCTION

Speaking is only one of the communication skills that we have. For most people there are four main skills: **speaking**, **listening**, **writing**, and **reading**.* Speaking is closely related to these three other areas. Speaking and *writing* are alike in that they both express our thoughts to others. Speaking is understood by *listening*, and speakers must use listening skills themselves to judge how their words are being received. Speaking a text aloud (one way of *reading*) brings the receptive skill of interpreting writing together with the expressive skill of speaking. See how closely these skills are connected?

When I was in ninth grade, I was taught that the first thing you should do when beginning any project or enterprise is define your terms. So that's how we start. Chapter One talks about the human voice and human language in order for you to understand the tools we have to work with so that each of us can find our voice.

Chapter Two defines one more essential term—the basic unit of speech communication, called an "utterance." Understanding what an utterance is helps us to understand how to be effective and considerate speakers. With that understanding, we can discuss the kind of speech we all use every day: conversation, the subject for the rest of the chapter. Chapter Two also covers guidelines and hints for face-to-face conversation, phone conversation, and the newest form of conversation, instant messaging.

Chapter Three explores reading aloud—a special kind of speaking that depends on a text. From an understanding of different kinds of texts, the chapter moves on to consider how texts make meaning, and step-by-step preparation for reading aloud, plus hints for "cold" reading, it you have to read with no prep time.

Chapter Four teaches you how to compose a speech from the first steps right up to the finished product. Some people might think creating a speech is a writing process, but it is actually best done as an oral process, and you'll learn why in this chapter.

*Members of the Deaf community in America use American Sign Language (ASL) to communicate. In this book, we will refer occasionally to the communication skill of signing.

In Chapter Five you'll learn how to practice and perform material, whether texts by someone else that you're reading aloud, prepared speeches, or speeches you have to give on the spot with little or no prep time.

When you're done, you'll have learned more about speaking casually and formally, about speaking with close friends and for audiences of people you don't know, about bringing to life words of other people and words you wrote yourself, and about making up words right on the spot.

Henry David Thoreau says in his book *Walden,* "Could a greater miracle take place than for us to look through each other's eyes for an instant?" When we speak to others, we give them an opportunity to look through our eyes—we share our world with them, and open ourselves to their response. I hope that this book helps you to use your voice to truly connect to other people.

Web addresses change!

You should be aware that addresses on the World Wide Web are constantly changing. Although the addresses provided were current when this book was written, sooner or later, some of the addresses may no longer work. If you should come across a web address (URL) that no longer appears to be valid, either because the site no longer exists or because the address has changed, either **shorten the URL** or do a **key word search** on the subject matter or topic.

To shorten the URL, **delete the end of the URL up to the first single slash** that appears after the colon at the beginning of the address and press the ENTER or RETURN key on your keyboard. (This slash often, but not always, follows immediately after a three-character extension, often .com/ .net/ .org/ .edu/ .gov/) This will usually get you to the home page of the Web site; from there, you may find a site map to help you or you may be able to contact the webmaster to find out about the page you're looking for.

To do a key word search, if you're interested in finding an American English dictionary, for example, do a search for the phrase *American English dictionary* with quotes around it, either on your favorite search engine or entered into the "Go To" or "Address" box on your browser. Many search engines list the top-rated sites first, so check the blurb about the top site, and if it seems good, try it out.

WARNING: Not every response to your search will match your criteria, and some sites may contain adult material. If you are ever in doubt, check with someone who can help you.

CHAPTER ONE

Finding Your Voice

ELEMENTS OF THE VOICE

Can you tell a horse's neigh from a tiger's roar? A clarinet's trill from a bass drum's boom? Bugs Bunny's wisecracks from Tweety's chirpy comments? Can you recognize your favorite singer by his or her voice?

When we identify a sound or a voice, we often can't say exactly how we did it. But as we begin to study the art of speaking and start to make conscious choices about how we use our voices, being able to identify the elements that make up voiced sound will help us to understand how we can use our own voices more creatively and more successfully. The process of shaping words with our attitudes and emotions through our voices is called **intonation**.

ELEMENTS OF INTONATION IN THE VOICE

Element	Definition
volume	how loud or soft the voice is
stress	the amount of emphasis we place on each syllable
pitch	how high or low the sound is
tempo	how quickly or slowly we produce sounds
tone	the element of voice that reflects our attitude toward the content of what we're saying
pauses	silence between sounds to create meaning, leave time for breathing, build suspense, create rhythm, and so on
timbre	the personality in our voice; the characteristics that make our voice uniquely ours
content	the thoughts, ideas, and emotions expressed by our words

All these elements are involved whenever we speak. We use all of them all the time.

Volume is pretty easy to understand. We even have words like *shout* and *whisper* that convey not only that someone is speaking but also at what volume.

Stress is sometimes called accent, but we want to be careful not to confuse it with the meaning of *accent* that refers to the pronunciation of a language by a nonnative speaker.

Pitch changes with age (young children have higher pitched voices; young men's voices lower at puberty) and also with the content of what is being said. In English, we often signal statements by lowering pitch at the end, and we often signal questions by raising pitch at the end.

Tempo varies with context. We speak more slowly to people who are just acquiring our language, when it is very important that we be understood precisely, and in formal situations.

Tone is easiest to understand by looking at examples. This chart may be useful when you're trying to identify the tone of literature selections, too.

TONES OF VOICE

General category	Specific tone		
instructional	critical	explanatory	thoughtful
truthful	frank	innocent	sincere
persuasive	argumentative	coaxing	pleading
pleasant	approving	forgiving	peaceful
	calm	gentle	polite
	cheerful	gracious	sympathetic
	comforting	happy	tender
	compassionate	helpful	thoughtful
	content	joyful	tolerant
	courteous	kindly	trusting
	elated	mild	
unpleasant	accusatory	fierce	plaintive
	angry	flippant	pompous
	annoyed	frantic	querulous
	arrogant	frightened	reckless
	belittling	furious	regretful
	bitter	greedy	sarcastic
	boastful	grieving	saucy
	boorish	harsh	savage
	cocksure	hateful	scolding
	condescending	haughty	scornful
	contemptuous	horrified	servile
	crushed	hysterical	sorrowful
	defiant	impudent	spiteful
	desperate	insane	sullen
	disappointed	insulting	suspicious
	disgusted	intolerant	tragic
	dismal	irritable	uncomprehending
	domineering	jealous	uneasy
	egotistical	miserable	wild
	enraged	nervous	worried
	fearful	pitiless	

Continued

General category	Specific tone		
uninvolved	bored dull indifferent	languid monotonous nonchalant	sluggish
comic	amused facetious hilarious humorous	ironic joking mocking playful	satiric silly uproarious

Pauses were divided by the great Russian acting teacher Constantin Stanislavski into three types: logical pauses (dictated by meaning, rhythm, etc.), psychological pauses (used to convey the subtext of the words—see below), and breath pauses.

Timbre is hard to describe because we don't have many words to describe the various qualities of the voice that make up its timbre. We just "know it when we hear it."

Content does not really stand alone—it always exists in a context. You would likely express the very same opinion about the very same topic differently with different audiences, say, your best friend, your little brother, and your grandmother. Location can make a difference as well—what you say about an article of clothing to the sales clerk when you try it on for the first time in a dressing room is probably different from the way you discuss it with your father when he's asking you about the price and different from how you discuss it if you wear it to school and one of your friends compliments you on it.

Content includes the **subtext**, Stanislavski's name for "what lies behind and beneath the actual words," when feelings, thoughts, and imagination give life and intonation to "empty sound" so that "the word[s] becomes significant" (*Building a Character*, Routledge/Theatre Arts Books, 1977, p. 113).

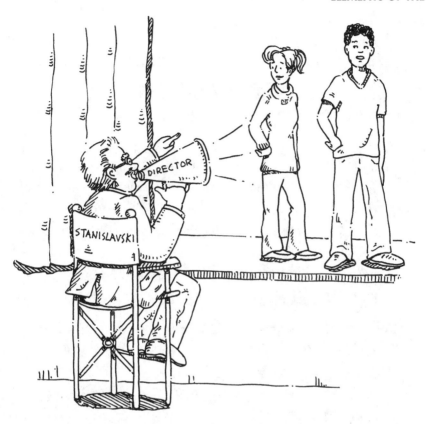

As we study intonation, you'll discover that each element that is changed, whether a little or a lot, changes how we sound, and can even change what our words mean to others. (A change in pitch can convert a statement to a question. A change in tone, from honesty to irony, for example, can make a statement mean its opposite.) But we are so used to making these adjustments in our voices that, unless we make an effort, we're probably not conscious of any but a few of the ways we use our voices to make meaning. When we speak thoughtfully, and especially when we perform (in a play, reading a poem, telling a story), we usually give the elements of voice more thought and use more variety.

BRAIN TICKLERS
Set # 1

1. Read the following sentences aloud in the ways directed. After you complete each direction, tell what element or elements of your voice changed and how.

It's incredible! It's astonishing! Oh, it's unbelievable!

First reading	Second reading
a. as if scared	as if enthusiastic
b. as if "it" is very likely unsafe, possible deadly	as if "it" is the fulfillment of your dearest wish
c. as if you are becoming more convinced about what you are saying as you continue speaking	as if you are becoming less convinced as you keep speaking
d. as if the person you are speaking to is approaching you from far away	as if the person you are trying to speak to is running away from you

2. Create a conversation in which you might logically say the following sentence: "We really ought to consider getting a pet orangutan." Experiment with the sentence until you find the intonation that makes you sound most convincing. Think particularly about which word you will stress the most.

3. Read the Gettysburg Address on page 265. How would you read it if you wanted to move someone to tears? Describe your decision-making process. Be sure to mention the eight elements of spoken language. Then tell the context in which you would choose to read the speech.

(Answers are on page 36.)

Voice production

So how is it that we speak? Well, there's a lot more to speaking than opening our lips and moving our mouths. Voice production coordinates our **breath production** with **vibration** and **resonation** and **articulation**. Here's how.

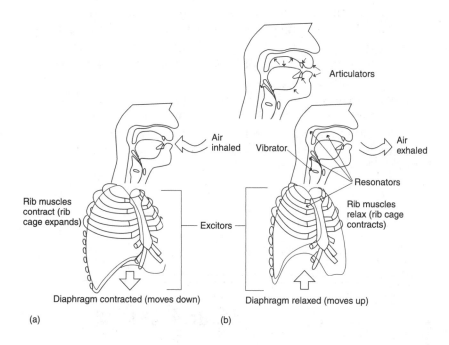

Articulators

Air inhaled Vibrator Air exhaled

Resonators

Rib muscles contract (rib cage expands) — Excitors — Rib muscles relax (rib cage contracts)

Diaphragm contracted (moves down) Diaphragm relaxed (moves up)

(a) (b)

You may already know that our respiratory, or breathing, muscles—including the diaphragm and the intercostals, or rib muscles—help us to inhale and exhale air. After we inhale, the **excitor** (the respiratory or breathing muscles that regulate or control the supply of air that we need to produce our voices) gets voice production started.

But we've all heard moving air—and it doesn't have the qualities of voice. How does it acquire these qualities? The air moves through a **vibrator** (our vocal cords), which produces sound waves when our breath travels across it. The sound waves are reinforced and amplified by **resonators** (the cavities of the chest, throat, mouth, and nose), which create the tone of the voice. The condition of these cavities affects how your voice sounds. If you have a stuffy nose, for example, the tone of your voice will be affected.

Now we have sound with tone, but this is not yet speech. We use the **articulators**—those that are movable (lips, lower jaw, tongue, and soft palate) and those that are not (teeth, upper gums, hard palate, and throat)—to shape each separate speech sound to create words. You are probably familiar with all the articulators except, perhaps, the soft and hard palate. The hard palate is the top surface of your mouth, commonly called the "roof" of the mouth. The soft palate is behind the hard palate and is used to close the passage between the mouth and the nose. If you say "ng" repeatedly with a pause to exhale in between, you will feel the soft palate lower to allow air to go through your nose.

It is important to realize that the vibrator and the resonators work involuntarily—we don't have to think about them. The excitor and the articulators, however, are under the speaker's control and need to be coordinated for speech to be understandable and effective.

BRAIN TICKLERS
Set # 2

Describe the process of voice production in your own words.

(Answers are on page 38.)

Air inhaled then Rib cage expands. talk exhale Resonaters work with virbration to produce sound

BEYOND THE WORDS

Conversation usually takes place in a context in which there are elements beyond the mere words. Usually, we see and hear the person who is speaking and can take note of facial expression, posture, gestures, movement, and so on. In a 1968 article for *Psychology Today,* Albert Mehrabian, emeritus professor of psychology at UCLA, reported that in a study he conducted only an estimated 7% of the impact of situations was verbal, while 93% was nonverbal.

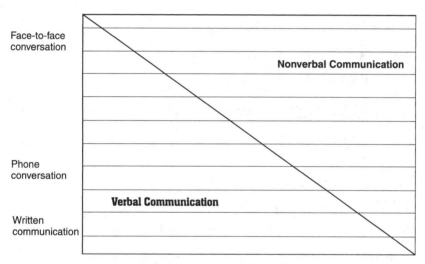

Each line like this _____ represents a particular conversation. Every communication is made up of both verbal and/or nonverbal elements, in varying amounts, depending on the participants and the type of communication. Face-to-face conversation tends to be toward the top half of the box. Phone conversations fall somewhere in the middle. Written communication generally falls toward the bottom of the box.

Nonverbal communication can either confirm or dispute what is stated verbally. When a person has inner harmony, his or her communication through all channels will give the same message. If a person is trying to conceal something, or is experiencing inner conflict, you may find incongruities or discrepancies in the messages that are being broadcast or may feel the discomfort that comes with inconsistent communication.

There are perfectly good reasons for concealing feelings—not every situation is appropriate for self-revelation, and we don't need to share our secrets with everyone. But in order to understand other people's communication, we do need to understand both their feelings about what they are communicating and their nonverbal meanings.

Speech reveals feelings

When trying to assess how people feel about the content of their speech, we pay attention to things other than the words they are saying. These elements are called paralanguage. Pay attention to these paralinguistic cues:

word choices that show emotion

tone of voice that shows feelings

unusually rapid or slow **tempo**

frequent and lengthy **pauses**

interruptions with nonverbal markers like "uh" and "mmm"

Nonverbal communication

We are aware of the elements of nonverbal communication primarily through our vision. Look for these cues:

Elements	Possible indication
facial expression	alert and interested or uninterested and distant?
posture	attentive or slumped?
gestures	usually indicate involvement in communicating
action	habitual action such as "bobbing" a foot or doodling can indicate boredom
clothing/grooming	is the person dressed for the occasion?

Incongruities and discrepancies

When you begin to study how others express themselves using paralanguage and nonverbal communication, you may start to see that certain things don't match up. Some of these incongruities you can only identify if you know the person really well.

what the person **thinks**	vs.	what the person **says**
what the person **says**	vs.	what the person **does**
how the person **feels**	vs.	what the person **says** or **does**
the person's **words**	vs.	the person's **nonverbal communication**

When you notice that things don't match, that what someone says doesn't jibe with what his body language says, for example—sure, he *says* he's comfortable, but the way he's twitching around makes it seems as if he's really unsettled— what do you do then? Well, that depends on the situation. You need to consider how well you know the person and what kind of connection you have. When in doubt, it's often a good idea to ask a trusted friend for advice.

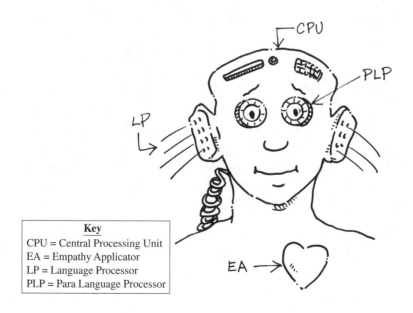

Key
CPU = Central Processing Unit
EA = Empathy Applicator
LP = Language Processor
PLP = Para Language Processor

Caution—Major Mistake Territory!

While it's important to be aware of a person's overall communication, it is also important that we neither overanalyze it (after all, most of us are not trained in psychology) nor take individual cues out of context. A person may be reacting to something entirely external to the conversation with you about, say, a joint project for your drama class: the person might speak rapidly because he is in a hurry to do an errand for his aunt Shirley, pause frequently because she is nervous about an upcoming exam in biology, or show strong feelings because his dog is having surgery on her shoulder. She may have forgotten to brush her hair because she was helping a neighbor rescue a pet cat. Use the information available, but don't be too quick to jump to conclusions.

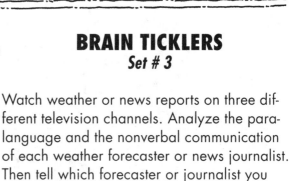

BRAIN TICKLERS
Set # 3

Watch weather or news reports on three different television channels. Analyze the paralanguage and the nonverbal communication of each weather forecaster or news journalist. Then tell which forecaster or journalist you prefer and why.

(Answers are on page 38.)

ENGLISH FOR ALL OCCASIONS I: LANGUAGE AND DIALECT

Defining language

What does it mean to know a language? It means that you can both create communication that has meaning that you choose and interpret the meaning of others when they communicate. This is true of both languages that are spoken and languages, such as American Sign Language (ASL), that are signed. To create and interpret language, a speaker (or signer) must know the sound system (or signs) of the language—the arbitrary symbols of the language with agreed upon meanings. *Arbitrary* means that there is not a necessary link between sounds or signs and what they name. For example, there is no good reason that the sounds made by pronouncing the word *mimosa* should name a particular kind of flowering plant. But they do.

Because you know the grammar of your language, you also know how to create new sentences that you have never heard before, and even sentences that have never been spoken before. Knowing your language's grammar also allows you to know what is and is not a sentence in your language. Nobody ever sat you down and gave you a list of all the non-sentences in English like this:

Journal Entries

38. Growing large purple dinosaur grape pudding never ever again.

⋮

2337. Love find me curling clouds wind in drifting music.

⋮

4619. Pry, sit, stand, soap, silly, slimy.

But you can tell instantly, without stopping to analyze or take them apart, that those collections of words do not constitute English sentences.

Dialect

If we all know so much about English, why do people speak it so differently? There are many reasons, and the first one we are going to talk about is dialect. **Dialects** are mutually intelligible forms of the same language that differ in systematic ways. Dialects develop when people who speak the same language are separated by geographical and social barriers. Changes slowly develop in their language—not enough to prevent mutual understanding, but enough so that each region has its own unique aspects.

Sometimes dialects are called **accents**. You may hear people talk about a Southern accent, for example. But this can be confusing because a person whose first language is not English is said to speak English with an accent, so we're going to reserve the word *accent* for this second meaning. Besides, a dialect actually involves more than differences in pronunciation (**phonological differences**), though these are important. There are also word (**lexical**) differences and word order (**syntactic**) differences. People who speak English as their first language come from countries such as the United States, Canada, Britain, Ireland, India, Nigeria, Kenya, the Bahamas, and Jamaica, so there are dialects of English in these countries, as well as every other area of the world in which English is spoken as a first language.

One important dialect of English *not* spoken in the United States is Standard American English (SAE), a dialect that is, according to Victoria Fromkin and Robert Rodman in *An Introduction to Language* (Harcourt Brace, 1998), "a dialect of English that many Americans almost speak. . . . SAE is an idealization. Nobody speaks this dialect; and if somebody did, we would not know it, because SAE is not defined precisely" (p. 408). African-American English (AAE), on the other hand, is a dialect, or group of dialects (including Black English and Ebonics), that is spoken by many African Americans who live in urban areas. Other dialects of English that are important in the United States are Latino English (spoken by immigrants from Spanish-speaking countries of South and Central America) and Chicano English (spoken by Mexican Americans in the Southwest and California).

Within dialects, **styles** or **registers** describe how people in a region speak in more and less formal situations. They are sometimes called **situation dialects** (as opposed to *regional dialects*).

CHARACTERISTICS OF INFORMAL AND FORMAL STYLES

Informal	Formal
contractions and abbreviations allowed	all words spelled out fully
slang, idiomatic, and colloquial terms allowed	standard forms and terms
fragments and run-ons allowed	standard sentence structure
fillers (*you know*) and pauses allowed	clear, concise expression desired
taboo words allowed	euphemisms desired

ENGLISH FOR ALL OCCASIONS II: CULTURE AND ETIQUETTE

What is culture?

Differences in dialect explain some differences in language use, but not all. In a book entitled *The Silent Language* (Anchor Books, 1981), American anthropologist Edward T. Hall discusses **culture** as an essential element in all communication. Because most culture is *acquired* rather than taught, we are not consciously aware of it—we have never studied our culture in a purposeful way, the way we have studied mathematics or electricity or the form of the short story. Our culture is like the lens of our eye—it determines how we see, but we can never examine it fully ourselves because to see anything at all, we must look through it. Thus, this most influential set of ideas that we carry and apply to life is beyond our conscious awareness, unless we take purposeful steps toward self-understanding. Encountering a different culture is, according to Hall, encountering "a completely different way of organizing life, of thinking, and of conceiving the underlying assumptions about the family and the state, the economic system, and even of mankind" (p. 23). So encountering a different culture may help us bring to light and reflect on our own cultural ideas because it may become clear to us for the first time that things that we took as givens are only cultural assumptions that—had we been born into another heritage—we would not have shared.

Take space. For people in the United States, our ideas about communicating across space are so consistent that they can be charted like this:

Distance	Appropriate voice	Appropriate content
very close (3–6 inches)	soft whisper	top secret
close (8–12 inches)	audible whisper	very confidential
near (12–20 inches)	indoors: soft voice; outdoors: full voice	confidential
neutral (20–36 inches)	soft voice, low volume	personal subject matter
neutral (4.5–5 feet)	full voice	information of nonpersonal matter
public distance (5.5–8 feet)	full voice with slight overloudness	public information for others to hear
across the room (8–20 feet)	loud voice	talking to a group
stretching the limits of distance (20–24 feet indoors; up to 100 feet outdoors)	shouting	hailing distance; departures

Adapted from p. 179 of *The Silent Language*.

Take time. Our ideas about time *certainly* influence our communication. In the United States, what we consider "punctuality"—that is, being no more than 3 to 4 minutes later than agreed—is highly valued. In other cultures, time is not viewed in the same way. It *is not* that people in other cultures are lazy, slow, or uncaring. It *is* that they have different conceptions of time. But, as you may imagine, when you gather people from different cultures together in a workplace, these different conceptions of time may create major misunderstandings and miscommunications primarily because, unless someone calls our attention to it, we have no reason to imagine that our way of see-ing things is not THE RIGHT WAY, THE ONLY WAY. But it's not. It's our culture's way. Unless we become extraordinarily aware of our own cultural lens, all our experience will be mediated through that one lens.

For information about cross-cultural communication, try these web sites:

"Business, culture, customs, and etiquette"

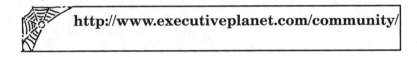

http://www.executiveplanet.com/community/

"Etiquette in other countries"

http://jobsearch.about.com/cs/etiquette/index.htm

BRAIN TICKLERS
Set # 4

1. For each of the eight distances in the space chart (page 19), write a situation in which you would speak to someone comfortably at that distance.
2. Respond to the following questions about five key elements (in boldface type) of communication that different cultures view differently.
   a. Do you and those you communicate with share ideas about **punctuality**?

If not, what are the differing approaches to time? How might accommodations be made?

b. Can you and those you communicate with find comfortable **spacing** when you communicate so that you each feel that you're at a good distance? If not, can you find another spot to talk in which you might be more comfortable?

c. How do you use **tone of voice** and **gestures**? Have your tone or gestures ever been problematic for those with whom you communicate? Is there anything in your repertoire (list of techniques and approaches) that you'd like to change?

d. What are your assumptions about **fun** and **humor** that enter into communication? Do those you communicate with share your views? Is there anything you could do to make sure that fun is fun for everyone involved?

e. Do you or how do you communicate about **deeply held beliefs**? If you don't, think about what others are missing in knowing you by not knowing about this facet of your life. Are you able to discuss things that are important to you comfortably with others who don't hold the same views that you do?

(Answers are on page 38.)

Genderlect: Does culture go deeper?

Did you ever think that talking to boys (if you're a girl) or girls (if you're a boy) was (a) nearly impossible or (b) doomed to failure? Linguistics professor Deborah Tannen (*You Just Don't Understand: Women and Men in Conversation*, Ballantine Books, N.Y., 1990) claims that cultural divisions go beyond those of region, ethnic group, and class, and actually include gender. Not only are there dialects, says Tannen, but there are also genderlects. Tannen suggests that only by taking a cross-cultural approach to speech between males and females can we understand the kinds of communication failures that occur. That is, if we think about men and women—even if they grew up on the same street, in the same town, with the same ethnic background—as coming from different cultures and approach breakdowns in communication between them as being culturally based, we are more likely to be able to find and deal with the issues that are getting in the way of understanding.

BRAIN TICKLERS
Set # 5

Are gender-linked cultural differences affecting your communication? Respond to the following questions for an opportunity to consider four key elements of communication that may be viewed differently by men and women.

a. What assumptions do you have about the roles of men and women that might be shaping your communication with people of the other gender in ways you haven't considered previously?

b. Tannen claims that women generally use language for connection and intimacy, while men generally use language for status and independence. Generally, according to Tannen, women see a lack of conversation as a lack of connection or rapport. Men, on the other hand, generally use talking to get and keep attention, says Tannen (pp. 76–77). Does this match your experience? Explain.

c. Do you ever discuss the way(s) you communicate or how your friendship or relationship is going? What advantages can you see in doing so? Why might it be uncomfortable?

d. Tannen explains that different people have different ideas about overlapping words in conversations, and very rarely does a conversation happen without somebody's words overlapping with somebody else's. But what some people can tolerate with ease and see as evidence of involvement and participation, other people feel as unbearable interruption. How do you feel about overlapping talk? Are you sensitive to other people's attitudes about it when they're speaking and you overlap with them? Sometimes it can seem important to interject a comment or question for clarification so that, for example, something is not left out. Do you try to make sure that your interjections move the conversation forward?

(Answers are on page 39.)

Etiquette

When we think of etiquette, the "magic" words *please* and *thank you* may be the first thing that comes to mind—phrases we learned at a very young age to smooth social interactions with peers and adults alike. But it is possible to understand conversational etiquette in a much more complete and sophisticated way. We could start from the very basis of human relationships: **respect**, **truth**, and **trust**. Later, when we get to know a person, we are free to rescind our respect, conceal the truth, and withdraw our trust if our best judgment tells us we should do so. But without being incautious, we will have the best chance of building a strong connection or a lasting relationship if we plant truth, trust, and respect firmly at the foundation.

So in the spirit of these three guidelines, we will find that there is a time to speak and a time to listen—this means both reciprocity (we each give and we each take) and turn-taking (no one uses up all the time or attention). If we follow these guidelines, we will also usually make time for civilities—as fits our own and our conversation partner's gender, dialect, and culture, and the level of formality that fits the situation. **Civilities** are the polite acts and expressions that help us move in and out of social situations and smooth interactions when things are uncomfortable. Generally we greet a person when we first see them (*hello, good morning, what's up?, ¿que tal?*), and speak words of parting (*goodbye, so long, later, au revoir*) when we leave. Usually we take care of what's most important first, which may mean personal items before "business" or vice versa, depending on the situation. We often continue threads of conversation that have been important between us in the past and introduce new items that we know or believe to be of interest. We apologize if we've done something that we feel uncomfortable about, or if we've caused discomfort for someone else. And we're considerate of the other person's time frame and agenda.

Cooperative conversation

Herbert Paul Grice, professor at Oxford and University of California, Berkeley, in an essay "Logic and Conversation" (*Studies in the Way of Words*, Harvard UP, 1989), proposed a cooperative principle for conversation that can help conversation participants create a mutually satisfying exchange. The cooperative principle states: "Make your conversational contribution such as is required, at the stage at which it occurs, by the accepted purpose or direction of the talk exchange in which you are engaged" (p. 26). This just means that our contributions to conversation should be guided by the conversational context. How do we do this? Grice proposes four categories of cooperation to guide people in being considerate conversationalists. In each category he suggests one or more maxims (pp. 26–27).

MAXIMS OF CONVERSATION

Categories	Maxims
Quantity	1. Make your contribution as informative as is required (for the current purposes of your exchange). 2. Do not make your contribution more informative than is required.
Quality	Try to make your contribution one that is true. 1. Do not say what you believe to be false. 2. Do not say that for which you lack adequate evidence.

Continued

Categories	Maxims
Relation (of material to conversation)	Be relevant.
Manner	Be perspicuous. [plainspoken] 1. Avoid obscurity of expression. [Use words your audience knows.] 2. Avoid ambiguity. [Don't say things that could be easily misunderstood.] 3. Be brief (Avoid unnecessary prolixity*). 4. Be orderly.

*Prolixity means unnecessary length.

Caution—Major Mistake Territory!

Just because these suggestions are in language pertaining to conversation, doesn't mean that you can't apply them equally to other kinds of communication. Consider them for speeches, interviews, and letter writing, among other uses.

HELPFUL HINT

When communicating with someone through an interpreter—whether your conversation partner is using a spoken language you are not fluent in or a signed language—remember to always look at the person with whom you are having the conversation, NOT at the interpreter, even though your eyes will naturally be drawn to the person who is speaking the language you recognize. This is an important etiquette rule for working with interpreters. It is appropriate to thank the interpreter at the conclusion of the conversation.

MODES OF COMMUNICATION

In 1983, in a book called *Frames of Mind*, Professor Howard Gardner of Harvard University introduced his theory of multiple intelligences. He proposed that, rather than a single kind of intelligence that people either possess or don't, there are actually seven kinds of intelligence:

- linguistic (verbal)
- musical
- logical-mathematical
- spatial
- bodily-kinesthetic
- interpersonal (understanding other people)
- intrapersonal (understanding one's own inner life)

With Gardner's work, more people began to understand that it isn't just a question of being "smart" or "not smart," and that school is not the only arena in which intelligence can play a role.

When speaking about communication, it is useful to employ a different set of capabilities that overlap with some of Gardner's: the three **performance modes**. Because we think about communication as being perceived through hearing and seeing, we look for a match between those senses and the ways in which people can communicate. There is an obvious match between hearing and the voice. But what we can *see* falls into several areas—we can see movement and action, but we can also see facial expressions that signal emotion. The chart shows the

relationship between our senses, our capabilities as communicators, and Gardner's intelligences.

RELATING THE SEVEN INTELLIGENCES TO THE THREE PERFORMANCE MODES

Sense	Name of performance mode	Intelligence(s) used by speaker*	Intelligence(s) used by listener*
hearing	hearing/vocal	linguistic	linguistic
seeing—movement	kinesthetic	bodily-kinesthetic	bodily-kinesthetic
seeing—facial expression	facial/emotional	interpersonal and intrapersonal	interpersonal and intrapersonal

*Other intelligences may also be involved.

Though each of us may initially be more capable in one or another of the three performance modes, it is an excellent strategy to become as competent as possible in all three modes in order to best communicate with listeners/audiences with different intelligences. And the same applies for listeners, who use the performance modes as **response modes**. Suppose that you are a personally intelligent person but are talking to a person whose strength is linguistic intelligence? Each of you, in turn, needs to perceive as best you can what the other is communicating in a mode that is not your strength.

BRAIN TICKLERS
Set # 6

To identify your dominant mode, use these questions to help you think about your natural tendencies. Qualify your answers if necessary. Create a self-analysis.

1. Do I learn best by seeing, by doing, or by hearing?
2. Do I express myself most easily with words, by actions/gestures, or in music, drawing, or some other nonverbal artistic media?
3. Among the arts, do I prefer to observe performances of music, presentations of dance, or displays of paintings or other fine art?
4. What problem-solving approaches and techniques do I use?
5. What do I find most distracting when I'm trying to concentrate: sounds, sights, or movements?
6. What do I do when I'm bored?
7. What memory strategies do I use?
8. How do I act in new situations? Do I look around? touch things? listen to what's going on?
9. How do I express myself when I feel strong emotions: with my voice? with my body? with facial expressions?
10. How do I best understand how other people are feeling? Do I rely on what they say? what they do? how they look?

(Answers are on page 39.)

INTERNAL FEELING AND
EXTERNAL COMMUNICATION

When we discussed incongruities and discrepancies (page 13), we mentioned that people do not always convey their inner feelings, and that sometimes it is entirely appropriate for people to be less than fully informative, depending on personality and situation. Now, we need to speak more carefully about this matter of correspondence between our inner feelings and our communication to the world. Looked at from one perspective, there are three ways we can speak: in our own person; as an actor, purposefully taking on a personality that is not our own; or on behalf of another person or organization for a specific purpose or project. Each of these ways of speaking brings up certain issues about internal-external correspondence.

Speaking in your own voice

We have spoken about **dialect**—the language that distinguishes people from different regions, and **genderlect**—the language that distinguishes men from women. But did you know that there is also **idiolect**—the idiosyncratic or uniquely individual language that distinguishes one person from another? Nobody in the world—past, present, or future—ever has or ever will use language exactly the way you do.

Idiolect

In the last two decades of the twentieth century, much attention focused on the criminal known as the Unabomber. For seventeen years, Ted Kaczynski anonymously let loose against university scientists and engineers with a barrage of mail bombs. The case was cracked and the terrorist identified when his sister-in-law recognized Ted's voice—in his writing. We're used to thinking about *voice* as meaning the sound of the spoken voice. What does *voice* in writing mean?

Don Foster, one of the leading experts in textual analysis—also called literary forensics when it's used to catch criminals—in his book *Author Unknown* (Henry Holt & Co., 2001), identifies elements of writing that make a person's writing unique and identifiable. Every one of these elements has a corresponding element in speech. This is not to say that people speak exactly as they write but to establish that we leave our fingerprints, or more accurately, our "voiceprints" (or "signprints"), on our communications.

ELEMENTS OF VOICE THAT MAKE UP OUR IDIOLECT

Element	Description
vocabulary	regionalisms, invented words, foreign words, characteristic interjections
thoughts	ideas and phrases used so often that their expression is ritualized
spelling/ pronunciation	the accuracy of how we convey the words we intend to communicate
orthography/tone	the look of our written or sound of our spoken voice
mistakes	our characteristic misspellings, faulty constructions, misuse of punctuation, etc.
punctuation; pauses	our characteristic use of punctuation or the vocal equivalent (see page 113), such as quotation marks, carets, cross outs, dashes, ellipses, hyphens,

Continued

Element	Description
For spoken works, add paralanguage elements, if applicable	
	commas, periods, semicolons, slashes, spaces, capitalization, exclamation points, question marks, and interrobangs*?!
grammar	pronoun agreement, sequence of verb tenses, avoidance of dangling participles, characteristic sentence constructions and mistakes, etc.
sources	use of quotations, ideas, and thought patterns as well as misunderstandings and misapplications from written sources, speeches, television, radio, movies, teachers, etc.
sentence length	long, short, varied—related to sentence construction and other grammatical choices
tone	see chart, page 5
facial expression	emotions shown in the eyes and face
gestures/gesticulation	use of the hands to convey characterization and meaning
movement	use of large body motions as in acting
stance	way of presenting oneself physically
dress/grooming	presentation of oneself to one's audience

*An interrobang is a combination of a question mark and an exclamation mark (called a "bang" by printers) used as the end mark for exclamatory rhetorical sentences.

BRAIN TICKLERS
Set # 7

Are you aware of any idiosyncracies—either habits of speech or choices—that make your language recognizable to others—anything that shouts *this is me!* every time you write or open your mouth? Ask a couple of friends to help you discover what makes your language unique.

(Answers are on page 39.)

Reflecting the Inner Self

It is when we speak in our own person that we have the most freedom to match our external expression to our internal feelings. Learning to balance honesty and genuineness with the control necessary to show respect for external situations and others' desires and needs is a process of lifelong learning. When and how and how much of our interior selves to reveal is never a question we can answer once and for all. Our belief in the foundations of respect, truth, and trust, and in the cooperative principle tells us that we should not give misinformation. So, in each moment, we decide what elements of our internal feelings we wish to communicate and either focus on the means to successfully do so or state that we do not wish to share anything at the moment.

At the same time, we know from studies of psychology that withholding expression of emotions can be destructive. To continually have feelings and either not express them or perhaps feel compelled to express contrary feelings can cause personal damage. If this is an area of concern to you, try to find an opportunity to speak to a trusted adult who might be able to offer some guidance.

Speaking in character: The actor in everyone

When we decide to act, we agree to portray with our bodies and our voices given material at a given time, regardless of our own personal feelings or circumstances at that time. Even though we may draw abundantly on our memories of sensations, experiences, and emotions to give our performance, it is virtually certain that at least in some part of our acting, we will have to present an external reality with our bodies and voices that does not match our internal feelings at that moment. In this case, when we do not convey our inner reality, we are not being untruthful, for we are, and others *know* we are, playing a role. Our performance should be judged, by ourselves and by others, by how well we communicated what we were trying to/directed to communicate—that is, by our acting skill.

HELPFUL HINT

The separation of internal feelings and external reality in acting does *not* mean that you should do something in a role that feels uncomfortable to you. If you find a direction unsettling for any reason, speak to the director about your concerns, and if that does not clear up the issue, consult another trusted adult.

Speaking on behalf of others

Suppose you and your siblings want to convince your parents to get a frog. Suppose you're elected student council president. Suppose you become a member of the board of the local parks and recreation department. Well, it could happen! And then you might end up representing the group in public.

When you speak on behalf of others, you often end up with a mix in terms of representing yourself—you may agree absolutely with some of the things you state and feel not so supportive of other things you find yourself saying because the majority supports them. It's like a combination of speaking for yourself and acting—and if it helps, you might try thinking about your role in this way. Some of the time, when your internal feelings match your communication, you can speak wholeheartedly in your own voice. At other times, when you have to say something that contradicts your personal stance, you may have to draw on memories of other times and project, not your own feelings at the moment, but the communication that you have agreed to give on behalf of the group—in other words, you need to act.

BRAIN TICKLERS—THE ANSWERS

Set # 1, page 8

Answers will vary.

1. a.

Vocal Element	Fear	Enthusiasm
VOLUME	soft	loud
STRESS	minimal	more
PITCH	high, squeaky	lower, close to normal
TEMPO	fast, no pauses	a little slower, pauses for emphasis
TIMBRE	not much air	full and hearty
CONTENT	same	same

b. First reading: I paused between each sentence, increased the volume of my voice for each one, and used more stress in each one. Second reading: I also paused between each sentence, but I slowed the tempo and increased the volume for each one, making the tone richer and warmer.

c. First reading: I increased the tempo and volume and stress as I went on. Second reading: I slowed the tempo, added pauses, lessened the volume and the level of stresses, and allowed my voice to weaken by using less breath.

d. First reading: I decreased the volume from a yell, to a loud voice, to a conversational voice, with a pause between each, and also in the first sentence when I yelled, I elongated and stressed every syllable, but by the third sentence, I was speaking "normally." Second reading: I reversed my approach to the first reading (starting with a normal, conversational voice, and getting louder). I also changed my tone (I decided to be puzzled about why the person was running away), except for the last sentence: Instead of elongating, I did it like hammer strokes with a strong, sharp stress on every loud syllable, until the last syllable, which I held for a bit.

2. Answers will vary. **Possible response** (context with stressed word italicized):

Mom: I'm really quite sick of Peter's everlasting snakes.
Eric: Me, too. I don't like reptiles. I don't like their scales.
Mom: I don't much care for his toads either.
Eric: Me, too. I don't like amphibians.
Me: I'd like a furry pet.
Mom: Yes, furry and cuddly.
Eric: Me, too. I like mammals.
Mom: I think I'd like something that doesn't eat rodents or insects.
Me: We really ought to consider getting a pet *orangutan*.

3. Answers will vary. You should note the patterns, including repetition of words and sentence construction; and the meaning in terms of the history of our country, and why the Gettysburg Address is still important. It might be appropriate to read this at an occasion marking an historic day, an event honoring our country, a celebration of freedom, or a remembrance of veterans and their sacrifices.

Set # 2, page 10

Answers will vary. **Possible response:**

After I inhale, my respiratory muscles move the air through my vocal cords, creating sound waves. These sound waves are reinforced and amplified in my chest, throat, mouth, and nasal cavities, and then shaped by my movable and nonmovable articulators into recognizable speech sounds.

Set # 3, page 14

Answers will vary depending on which reporters are observed at which particular time(s). Answers should include comments on word choice, tone, tempo, pauses, interruptions with nonverbal markers like "uh" and "mmm" (page 12), facial expression, posture, gestures, actions, clothing, and grooming.

Set # 4, page 21

1. **Possible responses:** very close—playing "telephone"; close—talking to a friend in the library reference room; near—planning a birthday present for my brother with my sister; neutral (a)—talking at work about something that happened at home; neutral (b)—talking at work about some work-related topic; public distance—asking a cashier for information; across the room—toasting someone on a special occasion; stretching the limits—calling family members in for dinner.

2. Answers will vary. Clearly express your own views and compare and contrast them with the views of those with whom you communicate. Then make reasonable suggestions.

Set # 5, page 23

Answers will vary. Clearly express your own views and compare and contrast them with the views of those with whom you communicate. Then make reasonable suggestions.

Set # 6, page 29

Answers will vary.

Set # 7, page 33

Answers will vary. The more careful the analysis, the more you will learn about your idiolect.

CHAPTER TWO

"Confer, Converse, and Otherwise Hobnob": Informal Talk with Others

HOW DOES COMMUNICATION HAPPEN?

When she was nineteen months old, after a normal infancy in which she walked the day she turned one and learned a few words (including the word *water*), Helen Adams Keller contracted scarlet fever, which nearly killed her and left her deaf and blind. Her communication with others became severely impaired. She not only lost the ability to speak and didn't learn any new words, but also lost the understanding of the use of symbols to represent things. But then, in one amazing moment, this understanding came back. In *The Story of My Life*, she tells it in her own words:

> Some one was drawing water and my teacher placed my hand under the spout. As the cool stream gushed over one hand she spelled into the other the word water, first slowly, then rapidly. I stood still, my whole attention fixed upon the motions of her fingers. Suddenly I felt a misty consciousness as of something forgotten—a thrill of returning thought; and somehow the mystery of language was revealed to me. I knew then that "w-a-t-e-r" meant the wonderful cool something that was flowing over my hand. That living word awakened my soul, gave it light, hope, joy, set it free!

The complete text of *The Story of My Life*, as well as some of Helen Keller's letters, is available at:

 http://www.textlibrary.com/download/storyofm.txt

BRAIN TICKLERS
Set # 8

Write a brief essay telling the importance words and communication have had in your life.

(Answer is on page 84.)

A moment of understanding

Helen Keller's recollections allow us to see the smallest complete instance of communication—a moment of understanding. This particular moment—Helen's recognition of the connection between the word *water* and the substance water—so fascinated Louisiana essayist/novelist Walker Percy that he tried to draw it as a general principle (see Diagram 1). I've included a redrawing of his diagram (Diagram 2) to make it easier to understand.

Diagram 2 shows what a successful moment of communication means. The identification that one person makes between an object and a symbol representing that object is identically perceived by the other person. The two people are "of one mind." They understand each other.

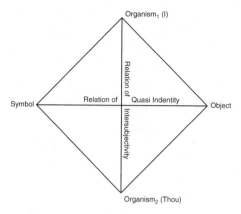

Diagram 1

Percy's Diagram from his essay "Semiotic and a Theory of Knowledge" is called *The Intentional Relation of Identity.*

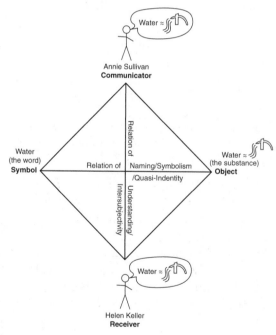

Diagram 2

Percy's Diagram made easier

But even this simple kind of communication can go wrong. Here's how:

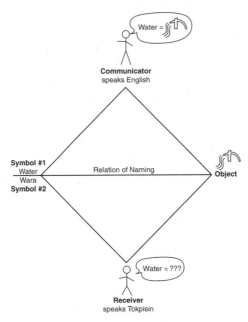

Diagram 3
Receiver and Communicator have different symbols for the same object **OR** Communicator is not paying attention to meeting Receiver's needs.

Diagram 3 shows two people who speak different languages, so they use different words (symbols) to refer to the same object. But you could have the same problem with people who speak the same language. Twelve native speakers of American English could misunderstand each other because they refer to one and the same sandwich by the following twelve different names: bomber, grinder, hero, hoagie, Cuban sandwich, Italian sandwich, muffuletta, poor boy, sub, torpedo, wedge, zep.

HELPFUL HINT

Sometimes you can prevent this kind of misunderstanding by thinking things out. If you're speaking to someone whom you know has a limited vocabulary (say a young child) you can try to choose words that will be easily understood.

You'll never know all the words someone else uses and doesn't use. But you can learn to recognize signs of confusion which usually come in three flavors:

- facial expression (frown, puzzlement, looking lost)
- verbal expression (direct questioning or noises like *huh?*)
- body language

If you think someone doesn't understand what you said, the best thing to do is stop and ask.

Diagram 4 shows a misunderstanding that results from the similar sound of words or phrases in different languages, but this could happen to two people speaking the same language. It can result from small glitches in pronunciation, background noise or other distractions, or misconstrued context. I could be talking about my brother Barry, and you could be thinking I was referring to our mutual friend Perry.

Diagram 5 shows a misunderstanding that results from the communicator and the receiver being on entirely different tracks. Maybe the receiver didn't hear what the communicator said, or maybe the receiver doesn't care. In either case, there isn't any connection between them. It's not even clear that the receiver knows that the communicator is trying to say something. This is a complete communication failure.

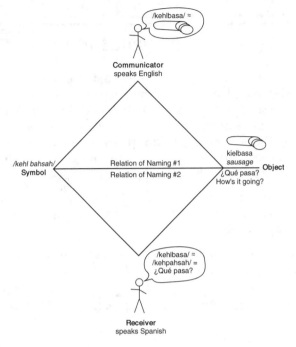

Diagram 4
Receiver and Communicator have unrelated words that sound close enough alike that they are mistaken one for the other, so they end up with different objects in mind.

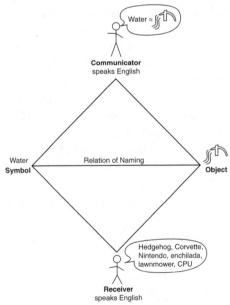

Diagram 5
Receiver is inattentive.

BRAIN TICKLERS
Set # 9

1. Think of or research three instances in which English speakers could misunderstand each other because (just as with sandwiches on crusty buns) they use different words to name the same object.
2. Create two conversations in which people mistake each other's meaning because of two words that sound nearly or exactly alike. Your examples may use people who speak the same dialect, different dialects, or different languages.

(Answers are on page 84.)

There's a problem with this concept of communication we've been working with. Let's face it: Virtually all our communication is a lot more complex than matching a simple word or phrase with an object as shown in our diagrams. Take the three-word sentence, "I love you"—*I* and *you* may be perfectly clear, but what exactly does each person mean by *love*? And is it anything like the same thing? If so much can go wrong when we examine a communication that involves one simple word or phrase, you can imagine how complex the process of trying to successfully communicate fully blown sentences, ideas, stories, feelings, and philosophies may be!

Furthermore, communication doesn't happen all in a moment —it takes place over time and within the complex interactions of life. We need to develop a more sophisticated understanding to match the more intricate reality.

The idea of an "utterance"

You have probably heard that a sentence is a complete thought. We have been given this model so that we can distinguish sentences from fragments (fragments are said to be incomplete) as well as from run-ons (which are said to have multiple thoughts). But if you have ever tried to use this definition, you have—more than likely—run into problems because it fails to distinguish complete *grammatical* thoughts from complete *conceptual* thoughts. A complete *grammatical* thought has a subject and a predicate. A complete *conceptual* thought expresses the entire meaning that the person wishes to convey, regardless of whether it is grammatically correct or not, regardless of whether it is a sentence fragment or an entire novel.

Consider this communication, which according to the rules of grammar is a fragment: "Ouch!" Is it a complete conceptual thought? Yes.

Now consider this communication: the Gettysburg Address (see page 265). It has ten grammatically complete sentences, but this does not mean that it contains ten separate, conceptually complete thoughts. A little consideration shows us that those ten sentences were constructed with enormous care to convey one thing. Let's look at one of the sentences Lincoln spoke: "It is altogether fitting and proper that we should do this." If we consider the matter carefully, we can see that this sentence is clearly not a complete conceptual thought in itself because the meaning of *this* depends entirely on what comes before. If you think about it, most sentences are, *conceptually* speaking, fragments of a larger thought—few of them can stand alone as complete ideas.

Do you see what I'm getting at? This famous rule works for grammar and for forming sentences, but it does NOT work for concepts and ideas. And conveying complete concepts and ideas is the big picture of what speech communication is about. So we're going to put aside the old rule and substitute a definition that will help us gain a deeper understanding of communication: the idea of an "utterance" introduced by Russian linguist Mikhail Bakhtin and explained in his essay "The Problem of Speech Genres" (in *Speech Genres and Other Late Essays*, University of Texas Press, 1986, pp. 60–102).

The role of the listener

The first thing we need to understand is the role of the person that Bakhtin calls the listener. We have been calling this person the receiver because, in the single moment in Percy's diagram, that person's role was simply to receive and understand and because we wanted to allow for the possibility of spoken, written, or signed language (and please, although we're going to use Bakhtin's vocabulary now, keep thinking of the listener in this broad way). Bakhtin points out that the listener is not just a receiver—a passive participant as the diagram of the moment suggests. The listener, rather, is an **active respondent**. The listener may agree completely or partially with what has been communicated; s/he may disagree, again more or less; s/he may wish to add to what has been heard, apply it in a particular situation, and so on. And, most important, sooner or later, the listener will become the speaker: sooner or later, the listener will respond to what has been communicated—either in words or in deeds, either to the original speaker or to others.

Communication over time

And, if we think about it, we realize that this speaker we are talking about has been a listener in the past. In fact, this particular communication is best understood as a link in a long chain, or better yet, a complex web of communication that includes all the communications that the speaker and the listener have each participated in during their entire lives.

Don Foster (see page 31) claims in *Author Unknown* that "the mind of the writer (poet or felon, no matter which) cannot be understood without first inquiring after the texts, including television, film, and even music CDs, by which that mind has been conditioned. *You are what you read.* When you write, your reading leaves its imprint on the page" (p. 13). What Foster says of writing is equally true of speaking. And he leaves out what he may not have easy access to in his research, but what we must see as another phenomenally important source of influence on the mind of the speaker and a shaper of future communication between people—past conversations. Not only is it true that "you are what you read," you are also what has been said to you.

Utterance defined

Knowing the role of the listener paves the way for defining an utterance, which, claims Bakhtin, is the true unit of speech communication. An **utterance** is defined in part by its *boundaries*. This means that the utterance is preceded by the speech of someone else and followed by the speech of someone else *when the speaker ends in order to allow someone else a turn that is not an interruption*. It is secondly defined by what Bakhtin calls *finalization*. Finalization occurs when a speaker has communicated in speech or writing (or sign) all that s/he wishes to communicate at that time under those circumstances.

Three criteria let us know when finalization is achieved. The first criterion is the *possibility of response*. For example, a scientist does not respond in print to another scientist's research until the first scientist has written up that research. By being "written up"—no matter how much it has been discussed in conversation and interoffice memos—the research acquires a new, finalized status. Only then is it appropriate for colleagues to discuss it and respond to it publicly. The second criterion is *context*; the subject, the people involved, and their history of communication all create a particular situation, the needs of which must be fulfilled for finalization to take place. That is, my utterance is not finalized until I've told my story to you in the particular way I tell it to you based on our relationship, history, and context. This telling is likely different, maybe extraordinarily different, from the way I'd tell the "same" story to my sister, my editor, or my best friend. This is called the sphere. The third criterion is the *genre* that the speaker chooses (we will discuss genre more fully beginning on page 95). Each genre has a certain characteristic content, length, style, and compositional structure—for example, we know what to expect from intimate conversation and from a formal farewell. These expectations help us to know when finalization has been achieved.

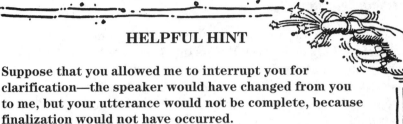

HELPFUL HINT

Suppose that you allowed me to interrupt you for clarification—the speaker would have changed from you to me, but your utterance would not be complete, because finalization would not have occurred.

We can now clarify the difference between a sentence and an utterance. A sentence is a unit of language. An utterance is a unit of speech communication. A sentence is complete when its grammatical form is realized. An utterance is not finalized until the full communication—whether it be a two-letter exclamation or a 1,000-page novel—is laid out. If a single sentence of a speaker is preceded and followed by sentences of another speaker and is a finalized communication, then that particular sentence is an utterance.

BRAIN TICKLERS
Set # 10

For each sentence or fragment, create a conversational context in which it can stand as an utterance.

1. Ah!	5. Ugh!	9. Yup.
2. Ouch!	6. That's true.	10. Great!
3. Take care.	7. Dunno.	
4. Huh!	8. Thank you.	

(Answers are on page 84.)

An utterance is meant to evoke a response. This doesn't mean that the speaker just wants the listener to talk back either.

SOME WAYS YOU CAN RESPOND TO AN UTTERANCE

affirm it	discuss it	relate it to other things
analyze it	evaluate it	rely on it
apply it	examine it	reorganize it
appraise it	execute it	select it
arrange it	explain it	solve it
assess it	integrate it	summarize it
build it	investigate it	supplement it
build on it	practice it	support it
buy it	presuppose it	teach it
categorize it	produce it	translate it
consider it	prove it	use it
criticize it	quote it	verify it
demonstrate it	rank it	weigh it
develop it	reinterpret it	

You might also cry, laugh, jump with joy, or hug somebody.

HELPFUL HINT

When you frame questions, think about the kind of response you want. Here are some simple points to keep in mind:

- One easy way to divide questions is into those that get yes-or-no answers and all the rest. If you want an explanation, make sure to frame your question in a way to encourage the style of answer you desire. If you're trying to avoid a long, drawn-out discussion, shape your question accordingly.
- If you ask a question about a principle or a belief (like "what do you think of or believe about x?"), you're likely to get a very abstract answer. If what you really want to know is about a particular context or situation, include the context and circumstances in your question so your listener knows that you have something specific in mind and can respond to that.

BRAIN TICKLERS
Set # 11

1. Identify how you have used five different responses to an utterance at one time or another in your life.
2. Explain in as much detail as you can how you once crafted an utterance in order to try to evoke one type of response in particular.

(Answers are on page 86.)

Speech genres

The complete concept or idea, feeling, or story in the speaker's mind or heart takes shape in different ways depending on the content, the intended audience, and the purpose for which the speaker is speaking. These considerations will help the speaker choose a **speech genre**—a form of written or spoken language in which the speaker casts his or her utterance in order to best communicate it under the specific circumstances. Examples of speech genres are novels, plays, weather reports, letters, essays, song lyrics, epics, textbooks, gossip, and horoscopes. (For more on speech genres, see page 95.) In this chapter, we are going to look at only one speech genre—the free-flowing, wonderful interaction called conversation.

THE ART OF CONVERSATION

Bakhtin's ideas about utterances can help us to be good conversationalists because he gives us solid criteria for evaluating when someone is done speaking and for helping others understand when we have finalized our utterances. To this foundation, we can add some of his ideas about how to treat our listeners respectfully. "When speaking I always take into account . . . whether [my listener] is familiar with the situation, whether he has special knowledge of the given cultural area of communication, his views and convictions, his prejudices (from my viewpoint), his sympathies and antipathies—because all this will determine his active responsive understanding of my utterance" ("The Problem of Speech Genres" in *Speech Genres and Other Late Essays*, pp. 95–96). By considering his listener carefully, Bakhtin hopes to prepare an utterance that is suited for the listener's needs, to make the communication as smooth as possible. He draws on his **prior knowledge** of his listener to inform his decisions.

Looking from the same perspective

Another way in which we can be good conversationalists is to try to match our perspective to that of our listener. There are several ways in which we can do this, both figuratively and literally: by being aware of presuppositions, point of view, and levels of engagement.

Presuppositions

A *pre*supposition is an assumption that's hidden in a statement and must be true in order for the utterance to have validity. There are many reasons that a statement could be invalidated by a false assumption.

The question, Who is the present king of the United States? makes no sense because it has been a long time since, at great cost, we removed royalty as rulers in our country.

The question, Who turned off the lights? assumes that the lights were on recently.

The question, Have you bought another iguana? makes no sense unless the listener has already purchased at least one iguana.

The statement, Joan no longer grows musk melons, rests on the assumption that once upon a time she did.

When you converse, be aware of hidden assumptions that may creep into your utterances.

It all depends on your point of view: Deixis

Deixis (dike-sis) refers to the pointing function of words that are affected by context. If I say the words *my grandmother's darning needle*, we're not talking about the same thing as if you were to say those very same words because when I say *my* it means something different than when you say *my*. When **deictic** words are used, you need to know **who's** speaking, **who's** listening, or **both**, to be able to know what the words mean. Besides first- and second-person pronouns (*I, me, my, mine, you, your, yours, we, ours, us*), demonstrative pronouns (*this* and *that*) are also deictic. For **place deixis** words, the meaning depends on **where** the speaker is (for example, *here, there, these, those, yonder, front, back, right, left*), and for **time deixis** words (for example, *now, later, then, last week, next spring, tomorrow*), meaning depends on **when** they were spoken.

Levels of engagement

Another important aspect of good conversation is that all participants be involved to the same depth. Finding the same depth can require careful attention because the nature of human interaction is that we only see bits of each other's lives. We go away from each other, and when we come back into contact, we often have little idea about what has happened to the other person in the meantime. And we begin our conversations with what Don Miller, Senior Associate in political science at Melbourne University, calls **verbal readymades**—phrases that have been used and reused so much that they are habitual, that we hardly pay attention to them, that we barely expect an answer. But here's the thing—although sometimes the answer may also be a verbal readymade, a toss-off, at OTHER TIMES, the answer may carry a cue that the speaker wants or needs to get off the readymade track and have a *real* conversation—to really have our attention and our involvement because something really important or interesting or crucial or wonderful or devastating happened in his or her life. Cues to look for include a slower tempo, longer sentences, content that alerts you that something's up, unusual pauses, or a direct request for a conversation.

Orality vs. literacy

Speaking is far more natural than writing. Of the maybe tens of thousands of languages spoken in all of history, researcher Munro E. Edmondson claims that only about 106 have actually been written sufficiently to attain a body of work that could be called a literature. But because we're so used to writing, we may not have ever thought about the different demands of communicating orally as opposed to communicating in writing.

For helpful tips, we can turn to Walter J. Ong, whose book *Orality and Literacy: The Technologizing of the Word* (Routledge, 1988) contains a fine analysis of the strategies that work in situations in which nothing is written down.

Ong points out that when your listener walks away from you, s/he will only know what s/he can recall from what you've said. This obvious fact, when considered carefully, suggests some concrete steps that can help your listeners retain more material—or at least the crucial bits you want them to remember.

HOW TO HELP LISTENERS REMEMBER WHAT YOU SAID

Strategy	How to carry it out
Speak in patterns.	You can create patterns on the level of thoughts, words, or sentence constructions.
Incorporate mnemonics.	A **mnemonic** is an invention to aid memory. If you ask your sister to buy you shoelaces, a piece of orange poster board, and adhesive bandages, you could point out that the initials of the three items spell *sob* and tell her you will cry if she forgets to buy them for you.
Use repetitions or antitheses.	Pay attention to anything in your thoughts that has duplication, repetition, similarity, or opposition—and exploit it.
Use formulas.	Usually we want to avoid them, but clichés work for certain uses, and memory assistance is one.
Focus on the concrete rather than the abstract.	Concrete examples are easier to think about in the first place; therefore, they are easier to retain.
Encourage participation.	The listener who has been drawn into interaction is more likely to recall material.
Avoid complex analyses and many levels of subordination.	Any material that requires the listener to hold a great deal of preceding information and organize it within his or her mind makes recollection difficult. Such topics are more easily presented with graphic aids and written handouts.
Target your audience's level of understanding.	Although it's easy to look up a word, or even a handful of words, when you're reading in a quiet place, it's harder to grasp the flow of spoken communication if you have to keep interrupting to ask what words mean. Be a thoughtful speaker and try to be considerate of your audience's limitations.

Understanding the communication circle

Michael Shurtleff, Broadway casting director, said it so well in his book *Audition* (Bantam Doubleday Dell, 1978): "Communication is a circle, not a one-way street. You hear people say in life, 'But I told him!' as if telling *at* someone were sufficient. If he hasn't received what you've told him, there is no communication. It takes *two* to communicate: the sender and the receiver. The receiver has to acknowledge the message by sending a reply back to the sender, thus completing the circle before a communication has taken place. This imposes a constant obligation on the part of the sender to (1) make sure his message is clear and (2) check that the receiver has received it. And an obligation on the part of the receiver to (1) make sure he's heard the message and is able to *duplicate* it and (2) let the sender know he's received the message. ... Communication's not easy" (pp. 87–88).

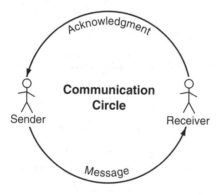

Taking Shurtleff's comments into account, we realize that, for practical purposes, unless we're talking to a large group, we should lay aside the link-in-the-chain idea of communication because usually it is most helpful for listeners to respond here and now so that speakers know that their communication was clear and effective. If all those involved in speech communication take responsibility for the communication working well, the burden doesn't fall on any one person—which it shouldn't.

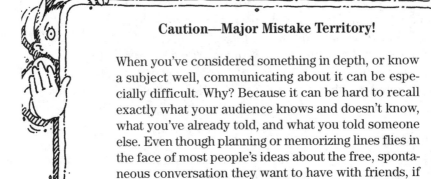

Caution—Major Mistake Territory!

When you've considered something in depth, or know a subject well, communicating about it can be especially difficult. Why? Because it can be hard to recall exactly what your audience knows and doesn't know, what you've already told, and what you told someone else. Even though planning or memorizing lines flies in the face of most people's ideas about the free, spontaneous conversation they want to have with friends, if you want to communicate about something that's really crucial to get right, you might want to consider doing some background work (you don't have to *tell* that you learned some of it by heart). Checking in with your conversation partner ("I'm not sure if I mentioned that . . . "; "Did I tell you about . . . ?") is another tactic that can help make sure that your whole idea gets across.

Maintaining a good attitude

And then there are responses that should be avoided because they have a tendency to destroy communication—to break the circle. Dr. Thomas Gordon identified twelve of them:

TWELVE COMMUNICATION SPOILERS

Spoiler	Explanation
criticizing	judging the person, the person's actions, or the person's attitudes
name-calling	using put-downs or stereotypes
diagnosing	analyzing in psychological terms, which most of us are not qualified to do
praising evaluatively	using praise as a stereotype, or in place of commenting on concrete accomplishments, artistic choices, and so on
ordering	commanding or demanding that the other person do as you wish
threatening	using the warning of negative consequences to try to force action
moralizing	giving advice in a condescending way by telling what should be done
excessive or inappropriate questioning	failing to respect another person's boundaries
advising	giving someone a solution, perhaps instead of allowing them to find their own answers
diverting	diminishing or dismissing the other's important issues
logical argument	responding with reasons that ignore the emotional content of the issues
reassuring	trying to stop negative emotions, whether or not they are justified

Since these responses aren't marked on people's sentences like labels on items in the grocery store, they can be hard to identify. What's more, people's reactions can be very individual. And with some response types—like praise, advice, and logic—there can be a fine line between what's appropriate and what's harmful. The best way to begin to learn about these spoilers is to pay attention to your own reactions when you feel others are being spoilers and to listen carefully if others react negatively to comments you make. And, since sometime or other each of us is likely to be hurt and, unfortunately, to cause pain or concern to another, it's important to be able to speak openly and carefully about feelings.

Talking about feelings

We can help deal appropriately with difficult subjects rather than spoil communications with negative responses if we can reach some level of comfort in talking about our own and others' feelings. For most of us, this is the work of a lifetime. One helpful tool is to have available words that name the subtle differences in the emotions that people feel. Then when you need to describe your inner state, at least you'll have a name for it.

HOW DO I FEEL?

absorbed	concerned	embarrassed
affectionate	connected	exasperated
afraid	content	excited
aggravated	crushed	fearful
angry	defeated	flustered
betrayed	despairing	foolish
burdened	disgusted	frantic
cheated	distraught	grief-stricken
cheerful	dreadful	guilty
compassionate	eager	happy

horrible	outraged	stressed
hurt	passionate	stunned
hysterical	peaceful	stupid
ignored	persecuted	surprised
imposed upon	pressured	sympathetic
intimidated	proud	tense
irritated	rejected	thwarted
itchy	relaxed	tired
jealous	relieved	trapped
joyful	rested	troubled
jumpy	sad	useless
lonely	satisfied	violated
loving	scared	vulnerable
melancholy	serene	weepy
miserable	shocked	wonderful
nervous	spacey	worried
numb	spiteful	

AFRAID CHEERFUL CONCERNED EMBARRASSED

MELANCHOLY SPACEY CONTENT SURPRISED

Three kinds of conversation

Conversation is an exchange of thoughts and feelings in an informal setting in real time. (The exchange of thoughts in a work-related setting can be more formal and is usually called a conference or a meeting.) A conversation is characterized by its back-and-forth nature. Unlike speech genres in which a single person holds the floor for a long time while others listen (speeches, sermons, lectures, etc.), conversation is marked by an exchange of comments. It used to be that face-to-face conversation was the only kind. Then, with the invention of the telephone, phone conversations came into being; with the advent of the teletype, people who use sign language have been able to participate in real-time conversation with other people who teletype or people who speak. Now we have Instant Messaging (IM-ing), which is a real-time written conversation by all parties involved. We will discuss the unique demands and functions of face-to-face, phone, and instant messaging conversation.

Face-to-face conversation

Sometimes conversation just happens. A friend comes over to you, and the two of you plunge into a familiar discussion of your families, favorite band, or plans you have for the weekend. It seems effortless, and you don't necessarily consider that you've "prepared" for the conversation, though, in fact, all the knowledge you've gained about your friend for the length of your friendship is coming into play as you talk.

When talking to someone seems awkward—when there are long pauses and moments when you don't know what to say—that's when conversation can seem really difficult. We're going to go over some hints for handling, even avoiding, awkward conversational moments. And, just possibly, some of these hints might help you expand your comfortable conversations, too.

Starting a conversation with someone you don't know

The first step is the easiest. You greet the person who has greeted you or with whom you wish to start a conversation and introduce yourself, telling all or part of your name, and perhaps some other personal information. Greetings can range from formal to informal, depending on the person you are addressing (audience) and the type of relationship you hope to create (purpose). How you introduce yourself will also depend on those factors. You also might want to state a reason for your interest in getting to know the person (this can come either before or after you introduce yourself). You might mention a mutual friend or acquaintance, an interest you share, or another reason that you think that getting to know each other would be mutually satisfying.

Caution—Major Mistake Territory!

Most times when you introduce yourself, you give your name. But there are times when, for safety, it's best not to. Young children are taught never to speak to strangers. But obviously, if we never spoke to anyone we didn't know, we'd never meet anyone new. Use your common sense, and if you're not sure, ask a trusted adult. It's okay to give a less than complete identification to someone you don't know if that seems to be the safest way. You can always tell the person more later, if you come to trust him or her. A mature individual will respect your desire to be safe and not be offended by your reticence.

BRAIN TICKLERS
Set # 12

For each situation, give a greeting, introduction, and a reason for getting to know the person, just as you might in actual conversation. Be sure to think about your audience and purpose and use wording that fits the situation.

1. It's your first day of physics class and you spot someone who you know is a really good student in math. You want to have a conversation that will end up with him or her being your lab partner.

Did you see the latest *Scientific American*?

2. You're asking the manager of a restaurant for a gift certificate for a fund-raising raffle.
3. You need to interview a politician for a news article for the local paper, so you're phoning your state's governor.
4. You see an adult walking down your street, looking lost.
5. You just saw someone do something illegal, and you're calling the police.
6. You're offering to volunteer at the local food kitchen on Saturday afternoons.

(Answers are on page 86.)

If you give a reason for your introduction, that in itself may get the conversation going. The two of you may go on to discuss the accomplishment, activity, or person that you've mentioned. If that doesn't happen, you probably want to have a **conversation opener** lined up ahead of time. Here are some suggestions.

CONVERSATION OPENERS

Topics of general interest	
news/weather	latest news items
	something pertinent to the situation you are both in at the very moment you are speaking
	unusual weather
newly acquired information	something you know that the other person probably doesn't but would probably want to know
A special interest	something that identifies you and that will make you memorable to your conversation partner and/or create a link between you
A question	something you really want to know and that will help get the other person talking
An opinion	what you think about some issue that your conversation partner might be interested in
A shared memory	something that you both experienced or know about

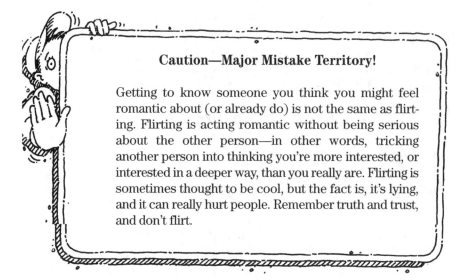

Caution—Major Mistake Territory!

Getting to know someone you think you might feel romantic about (or already do) is not the same as flirting. Flirting is acting romantic without being serious about the other person—in other words, tricking another person into thinking you're more interested, or interested in a deeper way, than you really are. Flirting is sometimes thought to be cool, but the fact is, it's lying, and it can really hurt people. Remember truth and trust, and don't flirt.

HELPFUL HINT

If you try to start a conversation with someone and the person is unresponsive, or actually leaves, it's best to let it go. Force is not a part of good communication.

BRAIN TICKLER
Set # 13

Think of a scenario in which you might use each of these conversation openers and complete each sentence.

1. Could you show me how to ____?
2. They're predicting ____ this weekend, and ____.
3. I think the new ____ is really ____!
4. Do you want to go ____?
5. Do you remember when ____?
6. Did you ever ____?
7. Did you hear about ____?

(Answers are on page 87.)

After the introductions

Once the introductions are out of the way, conversation can go, well, just about anywhere. Conversation is the speech genre that includes the most other genres within it. Flexible and spontaneous, long or short, deeply intimate, casual, or businesslike, it usually starts with a greeting and a question about a person's well being and ends with a farewell, but in between—the sky's the limit. Stories, gossip, reviews, reports, complaints, jokes . . . just about anything goes. We're so used to moving easily from one speech genre to another within face-to-face conversation, that we may not even give too much thought to just how versatile a form it is.

Etiquette in conversation

Occasionally it is necessary to interrupt a conversation. If someone else joins in (if the person has not yet met your original conversation partner, its up to you to perform an introduction: A, I'd like you to meet B. B, this is my friend, A.), you will need to save private topics for later. If your private discussion can't wait, you can excuse yourself to the newly arrived party, saying that the matter you're discussing is urgent and that you will talk with him or her later—or answering a quick question, if that's all that's required.

If conversation has to be cut short, it can be continued later—either in person, by e-mail or IM-ing, or on the telephone.

Phone conversation

There are some obvious differences between phone conversation and face-to-face conversation:

- no cues from facial expression and body language
- the possibility of less privacy and the risk of disturbing others with the sound of the phone ringing
- a need to be considerate of other's need for the phone (and if the phone line has multiple uses, for the use of the computer, for e-mail, for IM-ing, and for a fax machine)

Phone etiquette

Since the caller begins by being unidentified and since the caller can't see the person who answers the phone and may only have the word "hello" to go by, phone etiquette is particularly important to help people get connected quickly and easily to the conversation partner they are seeking. Some people choose to identify themselves when they answer the phone—it is always the practice in businesses to offer some kind of identification—but your decision to do so or not should depend on your sense of safety and your household policy. The caller should greet the person who answered the phone, identify himself or herself, and name the person who's being called—unless, of course, you already recognize that the person you called is the one who answered the phone.

Once you connect to the person you are seeking, the conversation proceeds pretty much as face-to-face conversation does. You just need to take a little extra care to listen carefully, since you will be relying on vocal cues to signal you about emotions, when an utterance is finalized, and tone of voice—some of the things you would have picked up from facial expressions and body language in face-to-face conversation.

Phone messages

Since people use the phone to communicate all kinds of important and urgent business, taking clear and complete phone messages and making sure the intended recipient receives them is very important. A phone message pad, a chalkboard or dry erase board, or any other agreed upon system will work. The important thing is that everyone who might take or receive messages uses the agreed on location and carefully includes the relevant information. The message should clearly indicate the following (and you can photocopy the next page to make a phone message pad, if you wish).

═··Message··═

MESSAGE FOR: _____

DATE: _____ TIME: _____

WHO CALLED: _____

COMPANY: _____

PHONE: _____ FAX: _____

E-MAIL: _____

MOBILE: _____

MESSAGE: _____

_____

_____

_____

_____

_____

MESSAGE TAKEN BY: _____

Instant messaging (or chat programs)

Instant Messaging is called IM for short. It is a free service that uses an Internet connection to link people who all have a similar service. Instant messages go directly from one user to another and are not stored on a server. This means that they can be private, unless they are sent to or from a workplace or institution that has monitoring software that captures IM exchanges. Therefore, where you and your conversation partners IM matters.

IM-ing is password protected, so you have control over who is in on your conversation. Chat programs are *not* the same as chat rooms, where people who do not know each other may gather in cyberspace. We do not recommend minors using Internet chat rooms without approval from a parent or guardian.

IM-ing is like being on the phone—just using typing instead of voice. You choose a screen name, and enter the screen names of the people you want to IM with—friends, relatives, business associates, teachers, coaches, and so on. Then your system lets you know when your chosen conversation partners are on-line and available to chat.

The length of an IM exchange is limited by how much text you can fit in the box on the screen, prompting the division of discourse into small chunks. It's kind to push enter after a sentence or two, not type a whole paragraph, so that your conversation partner doesn't have to wait for a long time. But this also means that (1) it's not the best medium for complex, well-developed ideas and (2) as exchanges go back and forth there's bound to be some overlap. Sometimes you may have multiple topics of conversation going at once, and this takes some getting used to and politeness as you work out who gets to have his or her topic discussed first. You need to pay attention to see when your partner's utterances are finalized and to try to give your partner cues to know when your utterances are complete.

Because of the shortened length of text entries and the need to send cues about message completeness (see eom and mtf in the chart), a set of abbreviations has evolved for IM (and e-mail) use.

Abbreviation	Explanation
adn	any day now
aamof	as a matter of fact
afaik	as far as I know
afaic	as far as I'm concerned
asap	as soon as possible
bak	back at keyboard (after brb)
brb	be right back
bac	by any chance
btw	by the way

Continued

75

Abbreviation	Explanation
bfn	bye for now
cmiiw	correct me if I'm wrong
eom	end of message
xlnt	excellent
fyi	for your information
gl	good luck
gr8	great
gmta	great minds think alike
hand	have a nice day
hig	how's it going?
iha	I hate acronyms
ihu	I hear you (I understand what you're saying.)
imho	in my humble opinion
imnsho	in my not so humble opinion
imo	in my opinion
irl	in real life (not on-line)
jk	just kidding
kit	keep in touch
khyf	know how you feel
l8r	later
lol	laughing out loud
mtf	more to follow
nbd	no big deal

Abbreviation	Explanation
np	no problem
nrn	no response (or reply) necessary
oic	oh, I see
pls	please
pcm	please call me
rotfl	rolling on the floor laughing
cu	see you
sys	see you soon
tcoy	take care of yourself
ttul, ttyl	talk to you later
tu, ty	thank you
thx	thanks
ta	thanks again
tafn	that's all for now
ttt	thought that too (when someone types what you were about to type)
tnt	till next time
tic	tongue in cheek
wb	welcome back (after someone has said brb and then come back)
?	what?
ygti	you get the idea

But where's the voice?

Since IMs are often used by friends, there's a lot of personal material involved. But unlike face-to-face conversation, there's no facial expression, no body language, and no vocal intonation. This can make the "tone of voice" hard to interpret. Is someone being honest, sarcastic, kidding around? Making a mistake about what someone means can lead to unfortunate consequences.

Fortunately, someone came up with a way to overcome the "blankness" of text. In 1981, claims Scott Fahlman, now a principal research scientist at the School of Computer Science at Carnegie Mellon University, he suggested that people label comments using :-) and :-(to show feelings quickly and clearly and to avoid arguments that were arising when people took sarcastic remarks too seriously. There are also claims posted on the Internet that the "original" smiley :) was invented and copyrighted in 1984–1985 by Stephen R. Cohen. In any case, since the eighties, thousands more of these symbols—now referred to as smileys, glyphs, ASCII art, or emoticons (a portmanteau word made by joining the words *emotional* and *icon*)—have been invented to represent more feelings, as well as characters and objects. Notice that you need to turn your head about 90 degrees left to see the smiley faces right-side up. This is true of most of these symbols.

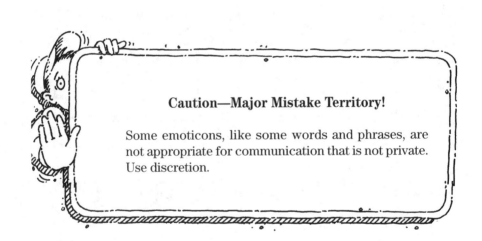

Caution—Major Mistake Territory!

Some emoticons, like some words and phrases, are not appropriate for communication that is not private. Use discretion.

HELPFUL HINT

In some programs, typing the keyboard symbols will convert into graphical images and faces, but this is not true in every program. You'll learn which do and which don't by trial and error. Other programs have pull-down menus of smileys—you just click on the one you want to insert into the text.

SMILEYS

Symbol	Meaning
:-D	big smile
:-|	disgusted
:-<	forlorn
:-I	indifferent or angry
:-&	perplexed
:-(or 8-(or (:-(	sad
<:-o	scared
:-V	shouting
:-\	skeptical
:) or :-)	smile
:-o	surprised
:'-(	upset or crying
>8-O	very angry
;) or ;-)	wink

Famous people/ characters/occupations	Meaning
=|:-)=	Abe Lincoln or Uncle Sam
O:-)	angel
d:-)	baseball player
Cl:-=	Charlie Chaplin
*<:o)	clown
(8<|	Darth Vader
>:-|	Dr. Spock (*Star Trek*)
[:-|	Frankenstein's Monster
7:-)	Fred Flintstone
(_8^(|)	Homer Simpson
****:-)	Marge Simpson
*<|:-)	Santa Claus
O-)	scuba diver
Animals	**Meaning**
:=8)	baboon
'''∧._.∧'''	cat
***	caterpillar
8∧	chicken
3:-o	cow or bull
=;=	dragonfly
6\/)	elephant
>-∧); > or <')))))> <	fish
- - -(8:>	mouse
3:]	pet smiley
:@)	pig
///\oo/\\\	spider
:<=	walrus

You can also personalize text with choices about font style, color, size, and typeface (roman or regular, *italic*, or **boldface**). And, of course, you can make up your own smileys and abbreviations.

IM programs often don't have very good set-ups for attaching files. We recommend that you send attachments in a regular e-mail program (check with your recipient to make sure that they can—and want to—receive what you send).

IM etiquette

IMs begin with a greeting, but not usually with a name, and they end with a signoff, but not usually with a signature—just like a phone call. IM-ing is informal and spontaneous, and people expect that mistakes in spelling and grammar will occur. If you do spot a typo in your earlier typing, you can't go back, but you can correct it in your next submission. Rather than correct the whole entry, you can retype your goof, an equals sign, and the correction. Or type "I meant ____." A smiley afterwards can lighten the moment, too.

With so many choices for conversation, it's important to know how to make a choice. IM-ing is cheaper than phone calls, and you can use it to keep in touch with people anywhere in the world—even if you're in different time zones. IM-ing is less interruptive to other work than using a phone or stopping to have a face-to-face conversation—you can do something else while the other person is typing as long as you pay attention to the signals (a flashing sign and/or a sound) that alert you to the fact that a message has arrived, so you don't keep your conversation partners waiting too long.

If a conversation partner indicates s/he needs to leave, type goodbye and get off. If you had something else important to say, you can always put it into an e-mail for him or her to read later.

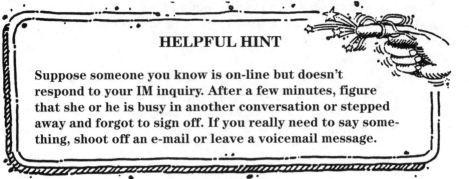

HELPFUL HINT

Suppose someone you know is on-line but doesn't respond to your IM inquiry. After a few minutes, figure that she or he is busy in another conversation or stepped away and forgot to sign off. If you really need to say something, shoot off an e-mail or leave a voicemail message.

In addition, be prepared for interruptions. Unlike phone calls, which take priority over most other activities, people feel pretty comfortable about interrupting IM sessions, partly because they know or suspect that their conversation partner can do something to pass the time while waiting. If you see the note *brb* (be right back) indicating that your friend was called away or had to shift his or her attention for a bit, type *ok* and wait for his or her return (or if you were in the midst of saying something, you can keep going). When your conversation partner returns, s/he will probably type *bak* (back at keyboard) or *back*, and you can respond *wb* (welcome back), to which s/he may reply *thnx* or *thanks*.

For your part, you can show consideration and avoid problems by using the built-in systems for signaling clearly when you have to leave briefly, when you have to end a conversation, and whether it's a good time to approach you or not. If your IM service has icons or alerts that let others know whether you are available, use them. If someone IMs you at an awkward time (maybe you're in a conversation with someone else), drop a quick note to say you're busy rather than leave your conversation partner waiting. If someone persists in interrupting you, you can use your program's blocking features to prevent the person from knowing what you're doing. If this is insufficient, change your screen name and seek the help of a trusted adult.

Another matter to consider is how formal the topic is and how important it is to save the contents of the discussion. IM vanishes when the session is over (unless you take steps to print or save a copy—even then it may lack information like date and time; check preferences in the pulldown edit menu to see if you can change settings). And you should give some thought to the value of the message. Most people still expect really valuable and important information to arrive by phone call or letter.

If you have access to IM in the workplace, make clear distinctions between your personal and business use, just as you do for phone and e-mail. It is best to have separate accounts for personal and business use.

HELPFUL HINT

Don't let IM-ing replace personal interaction, whether phone conversation or face-to-face conversation. People do IM with divided attention, and you don't have the benefit of all the cues that the human voice, face, and body give to thoughts and feelings.

BRAIN TICKLERS—THE ANSWERS

Set # 8, page 44

Answers will vary. **Possible response:**
   Since I'm a writer, you might think that communicating in words would be of utmost importance to me. But in reality, the expression I can make through music and collage are important to me as well. I value the wordless communication through color, texture, shape, and sound. Sometimes, like Eliza in *My Fair Lady*, I grow "sick of words." But eventually, I come back— I have to. Because for me, meaning is paramount, and words are one of the chief ways I make and receive meaning.

Set # 9, page 49

Answers will vary. **Possible responses:**

1. frankfurter, hotdog; hot cake, pancake, griddle cake; osprey, fish hawk, ossifrage

2. Native speaker of English: "Is that gouda cheese?"
   Nonnative speaker: "It's-a very good-a." (It's very good.)
   (This conversation really happened between me and a Russian immigrant.)
   I'll knead some bread (I'm going to make some bread from scratch); I'll need some bread (bread = slang for money—I'm going to require some money).

Set # 10, page 54

Answers will vary. **Possible lines that precede the utterance:**

1. Look, the fireworks are starting!"

2. "Watch your fingers!"

3. "I'll see you later. Have a good trip."

4. "Now isn't that just like Hugo!"

5. "The sewer backed up into my basement yesterday."

6. "I've never known Wilma to take a risk like that before."

7. "Is there any pizza left?"

8. "I saved you a seat."

9. "Did you find your stapler?"

10. "I'm going to Paris!"

Set # 11, page 56

Answers will vary. **Possible responses:**

1. Solved a riddle; verified a fact; refuted an argument; relied on an opinion about my health; explained an idea.

2. I once answered a single question with twenty songs and a brief essay to try to evoke consideration of a possibility.

Set # 12, page 68

Answers will vary. **Possible responses:**

1. Aren't you the person who won the science fair last year? I've been hoping to have a chance to ask you about your project.

2. As an eating establishment, your contribution to the food bank raffle would be especially meaningful.

3. I don't know if you remember me, but we used to play in the recreation basketball league together, and I want to speak with you about high school athletics in our state.

4. Can I help you with something?

5. I'm calling because I just saw someone cut down a tree on a national historic site.

6. I've been wondering if you could use any volunteers to help out with loading, unloading, or food preparation on Saturday afternoons.

Set # 13, page 71

Answers will vary. **Possible responses:**

1. Visiting a farm: "Could you show me how to get a duck egg out from under a duck without getting bitten?"

2. Waiting in line in the grocery store as the first week of May approaches in Vermont: "They're predicting a snowstorm this weekend, and I can't believe it!"

3. At the barbershop: "I think the new Vietnamese restaurant is really classy!"

4. Planning a date: "Do you want to go roller blading?"

5. Meeting a new acquaintance at a town celebration: "Do you remember when the town pool opened?"

6. Waiting for a plane: "Did you ever skydive?"

7. In line at the carwash: "Did you hear about the 2004 Corvette?"

CHAPTER THREE

"Once Upon a Time" Reading Aloud: Making Print Come Alive

Black marks on a white page . . . there they sit, waiting for a reader to come and bring them to life. Reading aloud to others can be very rewarding. It can influence people's opinions, stir people to action, move them to tears, lead them to reassess their values. This chapter will provide you with hints and guidelines to make the experience as satisfying as possible.

STARTING OUT WITH TEXTS

You've probably heard of **prewriting**—the term used to designate the planning you do as you prepare to write a text of some sort. But you might not think of reading as needing preparation the way writing does. If you stop and think, however, you'll realize that reading is a *very* complicated process. When we read, we have to

- recognize black marks on the paper as letters and words;
- process the words in groups to construct meaning and figure out how ideas are connected;
- relate the perceived meaning to what we already know about texts in general, texts of the same genre as the one we're reading, earlier information from this particular text, and so on;
- create in our minds the world of the text;
- apply prior knowledge of facts, experiences, other texts, ideas, feelings, sensory data, and the like to help us understand what we have read;
- try to recollect a new sequence of events and many facts and details; and
- fill gaps left by the text (no text tells absolutely everything that happened) with our own elaborations.

Maybe nobody has ever called your attention to the task of reading aloud and pointed out the opportunities you have to prepare yourself. So that's what we're going to do now.

Reading aloud is different than conversation because there's a text to guide you. Working with a text is a craft in itself because the skilled reader allows the many cues embedded in a text (as well as personal choices and the context) to guide his or her reading. The first thing we need to do is examine the world of texts so that we can understand the kinds of cues they hold.

First, we're going to assume for right now that you're working with an entire text, that is, in Bakhtin's terminology, an utterance. This is important to note because we're going to talk about the text with the assumption that it is finalized (that is, answerable), and that it completes the author's (and speaker's) desire to express him- or herself on the given subject in the given context to a particular audience at the given time. I will use the word *utterance* interchangeably with the word *text* in this chapter. And the word *listener* will be used to mean the one who both receives *and* responds to an utterance, whether the utterance is communicated in written, spoken, or signed form. To continue, we need to be able to talk about texts in a more specific way.

Classifying texts or what IS this piece of writing, anyway?

We can think about and classify texts in many different ways. I want to start by showing the limitations of some of these systems but also how you might get some good out of them.

Classifying texts by modes of discourse

You may have learned the names of some **modes of discourse**, such as narration, classification, description, and evaluation. Sometimes these are used as categories into which genres fit. So you may see a schema in which the mode "narration" includes works of history and biography, novels, short stories and so on. You also may have discovered the limits of this schema: that not every sentence of a story or joke or anecdote is narrative. There's a whole lot of description in these speech genres, as well as sentences—or even passages—of evaluation and classification. And not every sentence of a slide travelogue is a description of a place or its features—there's often a great deal of narrative telling the history of the place. So using mode as the main way of thinking about a text we're going to read aloud is not functional, although it might make sense to classify the mode of the text paragraph by paragraph or sentence by sentence.

Classifying texts by task

You may also have seen texts categorized by the **tasks** the writer carries out. There are texts that

- compare and contrast,
- define,
- list,
- sequence,
- argue, and
- classify.

Texts of any length employ multiple task types. For example, in a movie review, the writer might *list* the featured actors, *classify* the movie as a comedy, tell part of the *sequence* of the plot, *argue* with another critic's analysis, and *compare and contrast* the release with the director's earlier works. So using tasks as our main classification system is not useful either, although analyzing particular portions of text by the task can be most helpful.

Classifying texts by purpose

Some experts group texts by their **purpose**. They may also use the word *focus* or *aim*. Sometimes you will see categories of purpose such as *persuade, inform, express oneself*, and *entertain*.

But this schema doesn't work well for three reasons. First, we often have mixed motivations that vary depending on the demands of a particular section of the work, or we may want to accomplish multiple purposes with the entire utterance.

Second, in terms of composition, this analysis only focuses on the writer's attitude toward the listener (and in the case of self-expression, on the writer's self)—it leaves out all the writer's other influences. Any act of written communication actually has four major influencing elements: writer, listener, speech genre, and situation or context. One or some of the four elements may have more influence on a writer's choices than others in a particular utterance or section of an utterance. For example, in certain speech genres with highly defined structures (set poetic forms such as haiku, for instance), the *genre* governs the choice of each and every word in an utterance. When writing about a deeply emotional experience in one's own diary, the *writer* and his or her own thoughts and feelings will be the dominant influence. In writing a children's story for a very young child, the understanding and imagination of the *listener* will have an increased importance. And so on.

Third, this four-part schema fails for our purposes because only three of them (all *except* "express oneself") acknowledge a listener. And whatever part—large or small—thoughts about the listener play in the mind of the writer developing a text, someone who is reading aloud to others *always* has a purpose vis-à-vis the listener, which is to elicit a response from the listener.

SPEECH GENRES AND THEIR FIVE AREAS OF INFLUENCE

As it turns out, speech genres tell us far more about a text than structure or task or purpose. They immediately give us a set of expectations about the entire utterance in five important areas: the text's typical

- structure,
- style,
- content or subject matter,
- conception of audience, and
- range of purpose.

(Remember that *speech genre* refers to both spoken and written texts.)

Here is a list of some of the main speech genres you may find.

advertisement	anecdote	articles of incorporation
autobiography	ballad	biography
budget	bylaws	case history
chronicle	complaint	congratulations
contest entry	contract	conversation transcript
criteria	diagnosis	dialogue
diary entry	dictionary definition	editorial
encyclopedia article	epic	essay
fairy tale	farewell address	feature story
folk song	folktale	gossip
graduation address	greeting	guidebook
history	interview	introduction
invocation	invoice	job application
joke	journal	lecture
lecture notes	legal brief	letter
manifesto	mathematical proof	military command
mission statement	monologue	motion
myth	news article	nomination

novel	oral examination	parable
play	poem	praise
prayer	proposal	prospectus
report	research paper	resume
review	riddle	saga
screenplay	second	sermon or homily
short story	song	speech
state of the union	summary	syllabus
tall tale	textbook	toast
weather report	web-based user support	wish

Speech genres and structure

Some speech genres have well-defined structures that you'll recognize just from looking at their names (like dictionary definitions), while others have wide open structures that change with every enactment (like conversations). Structure is easiest to recognize in speech genres that have a **performative verb**. These verbs have a power over and above conveying or requesting or instructing—the verb actually enacts what it says. Saying a performative verb changes reality. Here are examples.

SOME PERFORMATIVE VERBS

Verb	Example Sentence
apologize	I apologize for my behavior.
baptize	I baptize you in the name of the Father, and of the Son, and of the Holy Spirit.
bet	I bet my lilacs will bloom before May 23rd.
bless	Bless your heart!
dare	I dare you to try.

Continued

Verb	Example Sentence
forgive	I forgive you.
move	I so move. or I move that (in parliamentary procedure).
nominate	I nominate _____ for office.
promise	I promise to keep this secret.
pronounce	I now pronounce you man and wife.
quit	I quit!
second	I second the motion.

Some speech genres share structures. Here are examples of how speech genres can be grouped by shared structural patterns. Notice that speech genres used in widely differing areas of life share similar structures.

SPEECH GENRES BY STRUCTURE

Structure	Examples		
Story structure: beginning, middle, end	anecdote autobiography biography epic fairy tale folktale	gossip history joke myth novel opera libretto	parable play saga short story tall tale
Letter structure: greeting, body, parting	diary entry e-mail farewell address	graduation address letter—business or personal	state of the union telephone conversation
Question-and-answer structure	interrogation	job interview	oral examination
Argument structure: state a proposition, offer proof	advertisement complaint diagnosis	legal brief manifesto	mathematical proof proposal

On the other hand, a haiku, the ceremony of changing the guard, and a second according to Robert's Rules of Order ("I second the motion") each have a unique structure that is not shared by any other speech genre.

Speech genres and style

Some speech genres may be created in multiple styles, while some limit the range of styles (for example, some speech genres are always formal). Some speech genres allow for more individual expression on the part of the writer (and speaker), while others are more restricting. Here are examples of speech genres that fit certain styles.

SPEECH GENRES BY STYLE

Style	Examples		
Academic	case history chronicle encyclopedia article graduation address	history lecture lecture notes mathematical proof	oral examination research paper syllabus textbook
Scientific	diagnosis	lab report	
Technical	assembly instructions	user's manual	
Artistic	autobiography biography epic monologue	myth novel opera libretto play	poem saga screenplay short story
Journalistic	editorial	feature story	news article
Colloquial	anecdote gossip	joke riddle	wish
Business	articles of incorporation budget	bylaws contract invoice	job application mission statement prospectus
Military	court martial record	military command	

Continued

Style	Examples		
Political	manifesto	state of the union	
Popular	fairy tale folk song	folktale horoscope	tall tale
Religious	invocation parable	prayer	sermon or homily
Open to multiple styles	advertisement complaint congratulations contest entry	conversation transcript criteria dialogue	diary entry dictionary definition essay farewell address

Speech genres and content

Some speech genres, like conversation, are amenable to any content. Others, like a diagnosis, have a very narrow range of allowable subject matters. This chart demonstrates that some speech genres, by their nature, allow for less range in their content than others.

SPEECH GENRES BY CONTENT AREA

Speech genre	Content area	examples
Award presentation	athletics crafts culinary arts	music science theatre

Continued

Speech genre	Content area	examples
	dance mathematics	visual arts
Contest entry	athletics crafts culinary arts dance mathematics	music science theatre visual arts
Event program	athletics dance	music theatre
Recipe	crafts	culinary arts

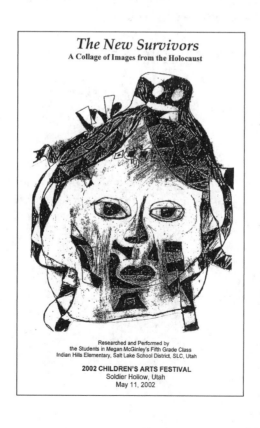

The New Survivors
A Collage of Images from the Holocaust

Researched and Performed by
the Students in Megan McGinley's Fifth Grade Class
Indian Hills Elementary, Salt Lake School District, SLC, Utah

2002 CHILDREN'S ARTS FESTIVAL
Soldier Hollow, Utah
May 11, 2002

The speaker's attitude toward the content (which will be revealed as the tone) also helps determine the choice of speech genre. We choose a parody, for example, to give our sarcasm an outlet, but prayers are unlikely to be sarcastic.

Speech genres and audience

Some speech genres might be adapted to suit any audience, but others are highly specialized. Bakhtin calls the speech genre's quality of being directed to someone its **addressivity**. The speech genre can distinguish the addressee by its level of formality, specificity to a certain occupation or cultural group, or application to a certain age, or the addressee of a genre may be more open and unspecific. The speaker can, and should, make further choices to mold the discourse to the actual audience. In reading the following chart, notice that if any of the members of the armed forces, any of the actors, or any of the executive directors also happen to be parents of infants or toddlers, we might conclude that the speech genres listed for young children should have them as an audience as well.

SPEECH GENRES BY AUDIENCE

Audience	Speech genre examples
Young children	alphabet books fairy tales fingerplay songs (like "The Eensy Weensy Spider"—or "Itsy Bitsy Spider" depending on your regional dialect!) folk songs nursery rhymes
Members of the armed forces	cadences military commands military instruction manuals military orders military regulations

Continued

Audience	Speech genre examples
Actors	audition announcements call back lists cue cards directions scripts
Executive directors of nonprofit corporations	articles of incorporation business plan bylaws employee identification number application mission statement

Speech genres and purposes

The purpose in speaking an utterance is to gain a response. We discussed some possibilities of how one could respond to an utterance on page 55. We can categorize these responses by asking ourselves if we want our listener to **act** in a certain way, **feel** a certain way, **think** about or consider something; or **commit to** or **value** something. Here's how these four categories correlate with the responses we discussed earlier.

CATEGORIES OF RESPONSES TO AN UTTERANCE

Categories of response	Responses		
Act	apply it arrange it build it buy it discuss it execute it	explain it integrate it practice it produce it quote it	supplement it support it teach it translate it use it
Feel	change adjectives in the chart on pages 64–65 into this phrase: feel ____; e.g., absorbed, affectionate, afraid, aggravated		

Continued

Categories of response | Responses

Think

analyze it	develop it	summarize it
appraise it	evaluate it	verify it
assess it	examine it	weigh it
build on it	investigate it	reinterpret it
categorize it	prove it	relate it to other
consider it	rank it	things
criticize it	solve it	reorganize it
demonstrate it		

Commit/value

affirm it	rely on it
presuppose it	select it

Now, here are examples of how the four purpose categories relate to some speech genres. It's not complete. Some speech genres are limited to one category of purpose, but many artistic speech genres can evoke all four purposes.

SPEECH GENRES BY PURPOSE

Purpose | Speech genres

Act

advertisement	manifesto
contract	military command
graduation address	mission statement
guidebook	nomination
instruction manual	play
lecture	proposal
lecture notes	prospectus
letter	sermon or homily
	textbook

Continued

Purpose

Speech genres

Feel

anecdote
ballad
blessing
complaint
congratulations
curse
diary entry
feature story
gossip
greeting
joke

novel
play
poem
praise
screenplay
short story
song
tall tale
toast
wish

Think

business plan
case history
criteria
dictionary definition
editorial
encyclopedia article
essay
history
lecture
lecture notes

legal brief
manifesto
mathematical proof
oral examination
play
report
research paper
review
sermon or homily
speech
textbook

Commit/value

business plan
manifesto
mission statement

parable
play
prayer
sermon or homily

BRAIN TICKLERS
Set # 14

The following are not complete utterances. So you will have to guess the speech genre from which each might come. Next, give your best shot at identifying the structure, style, content, audience, and purpose. Then identify the mode of discourse and the task. For 5, read the instructions and imagine how the dialogue takes place.

1. In 1900, colleges in the United States awarded 400 graduates with doctorate degrees. In 1994, more than 40,000 doctorates were granted. In the following year, 1994–1995, 65.1 million students were enrolled in schools and colleges in the United States, and in the country, an estimated $509 billion was spent on education for that school year.

2. Calico, with a lop-sided, black stripe down her nose, Sheba is my favorite of our pets. You would love her. She has long soft fur, and a sweet way of mewing to get attention if she has no more food left in her dish or wants to go out. But watch out for her temper! There's a sharp claw alert out in *this* neighborhood when Sheba's riled!

3. Dear Diary,

Dinner last night was a fiasco. As the saying goes, everything that could possibly go wrong . . . And I wanted *so* much for it to go well! How was I to know that Jeff had broken the box for the cornstarch and put it in the flour container? When I said I hoped I'd impress my guests, I didn't mean negatively.

Well, you might say, fortunately tomorrow is another day. Yes, I'd reply—the day I have a big Japanese exam. So I'd better say "sayonara."
Jenny

4. That on the first day of January, in the year of our Lord one thousand eight hundred and sixty-three, all persons held as slaves within any state or designated part of a state, the people whereof shall then be in rebellion against the United States, shall be then, thenceforward, and forever, free; and the Executive government of the United States, including the military and naval authority thereof, will recognize and maintain the freedom of such persons, and will do no act or acts to repress such persons, or any of them, in any efforts they may make for their actual freedom.

5. Instructions: Repeat what I say, but for the last syllable, say *key* instead of *lock.*

"I am a gold lock."
"I am a silver lock."
"I am a brass lock."
"I am a lead lock."
"I am a monk lock."

(Answers are on page 162.)

HOW TEXTS MAKE MEANING

Now that we've got some ideas about texts overall—we know about genre, structure, style, content, audience, and purpose, and we've looked at modes of discourse and tasks—where do we go from here? Presumably, after all this analysis, we've developed some fairly substantial ideas about meaning (for further thoughts on meaning analysis for four kinds of newspaper articles, see page 151; reports and personal essays, see page 152; stories/fiction, see page 154; scripts, see page 158; poetry, see page 160). So now we can narrow our focus to examine structure—how the writer has put the text together. The construction of the text abounds with meaning cues. And the more you understand about it, the more you'll be able to bring the text meaning to life with your voice.

Every text of any length has an internal organization that may include chapters, sections, paragraphs, or stanzas. Within those divisions, sentences are sequenced, and words are ordered within sentences. Words themselves are structured from syllables, and syllables are made of sounds. Through all these levels of structure and the way they are indicated on the page, the text's meaning is revealed and its performance is cued.

Orthography

Some things we gather from **orthography**, the representation of the words on the page in print. The spelling guides us in pronunciation. We may also gather what dialect the speaker is using. In this passage from *The Pickwick Papers*, British author Charles Dickens uses orthography to represent Samuel Weller's Cockney accent:

> "It won't do, Job Trotter," said Sam, "Come!
> None o' that 'ere nonsense. You ain't so wery
> 'ansome that you can afford to throw avay
> many o' your good looks. Bring them 'ere
> eyes o' yourn back into their proper places,
> or I'll knock 'em out of your head. D'ye hear?"

The apostrophes show the dropped *th* from the beginning of the words *there* and *them* and the *f* left off the end of *of*. Dickens also shows Sam's colloquial contractions (*ain't* and *D'ye*) and the substitution of the sound /v/ for /w/.

In this poem by poet Robert Burns, we see an example of the Scottish dialect.

> To a Mouse, on Turning up Her Nest with the Plough, November, 1785 (excerpt)
>
> 1   Wee, sleeket, cowrin, tim'rous beastie,
> 2   Oh, what a panic's in thy breastie!
> 3   Thou need na start awa sae hasty
> 4   Wi' bickerin brattle!
> 5   I wad be laith to rin an' chase thee
> 6   Wi' murd'ring pattle!
> 7   I'm truly sorry man's dominion
> 8   Has broken Nature's social union,
> 9   An' justifies that ill opinion
> 10   Which makes thee startle
> 11 At me, thy poor earth-born companion,
> 12   An' fellow-mortal!

Again, the apostrophe is used to represent omitted sounds. We can also identify lexical differences—*na* where English speakers from the United States would say *not*, *awa* where we would say *away*, *sae* where we would say *so*, and so on.

In *Little Women*, Louisa May Alcott uses orthography to show the pronunciation of Friedrich Bhaer, whose first language is German and who speaks English as a second language.

> "At efening I shall gif a little lesson with much gladness; for, look you, Mees Marsch, I haf this debt to pay," and he pointed to my work. "'Yes' they say to one another, these so kind ladies, 'he is a stupid old fellow; he will see not what we do; he will never opserve that his sock heels go not in holes any more, he will think his buttons grow out new when they fall, and believe that strings make theirselves.' Ah! but I haf an eye, and I se much. I haf a heart, and I feel the thanks for this."

Alcott substitutes *f* for *v* and *p* for *b* to show Bhaer's pronunciation of English and shows how he says "Miss March" by the spelling of the vowel in the first word and the final consonant sound in the second.

Typography

The kind of type that is used to form words, including the font, the size, and the style is called **typography**.

A font is a set of designs of the letter and symbol shapes in a particular size and style. Fonts that have little lines at the ends of letter strokes are called *serif* fonts. Fonts with lines that end plainly are called *sans serif* fonts. Fonts are used to differentiate elements of a text. Headings are generally set in a different font than the main part of the text—the body. Specialized fonts can be used to give character to certain words and suggest tone.

- Alleycat is a playful font.
- Times New Roman is a standard, respectable font.
- Geneva is a plain, no-nonsense font.
- **Sand is a casual font.**
- *Lucida Calligraphy is a sophisticated, elegant font.*
- Chilada Dos has ethnic character.
- FAJITA HAS CHARACTER, TOO.

The size of a font is often used to indicate importance. In texts with headings, the most important headings are set in the largest font size. The body of the text is set in a size judged to be comfortable for reading. Sometimes the first word of a section is set in larger, specially styled type to fit a particular page design, without suggesting that this word has special importance.

Most of the body of a text is set in roman style. The type you are reading now is roman. Two other styles of type are often used. *Italic type looks like this*. It is the same font as the body type, but it has a slight slant to the right. **Boldface type looks like this**. It is the same font as the body type, but each line is thicker so that the letters stand out. ***Boldface italic*** exists, but it is not often seen. Font style that is unusual (i.e., not roman) may give us hints about words that require special emphasis. We may signal this emphasis with our voices by slowing down and speaking the marked word(s) with special intensity, pausing before and after, and changing the pitch.

While boldface type is used almost entirely for special emphasis, italic style has several uses. It is used for certain kinds of titles (books, movies, plays, television series, court cases, longer musical selections, newspapers, and periodicals) as well as for the taxonomic names of genera, species, and varieties; the names of vessels, airplanes, spacecraft, and trains; letters; and words referred to as words. Either boldface type or italic type may be used to single out words that are being defined, that appear in a glossary, or that have particular importance in the text.

Capitalization is another typographical means of drawing attention to single words or short phrases, a way of indicating that the word is important and should be stressed. If it is used for longer passages, as in the novel *A Prayer for Owen Meany*, this is an indication that the writer has created a unique usage, and you will need to develop an interpretation on a case-by-case basis. Here is an example from *The Crisis* Number I by Thomas Paine, December 23, 1776.

> Britain, with an army to enforce her tyranny, has declared that she has a right (*not only to* TAX) but "*to* BIND *us in* ALL CASES WHATSOEVER," and if being *bound in that manner*, is not slavery, then is there not such a thing as slavery upon earth. Even the expression is impious, so unlimited a power can belong only to GOD.

Headings and other text divisions

Headings combine typographic and content clues to help us understand the organization of the text and the relative importance of material. Within a text, headings follow a consistent pattern from most important to least important. The pattern may include size, color, typeface, capitalized or lowercase text, and placement (at the left margin, indented, etc.). It is natural to pause before a new heading and speak it as an announcement of what is to follow.

The largest heading is usually the chapter title. The largest divisions within each chapter are shown by **subheads**. Divisions within a subhead are indicated by **sub-subheads**. There may be several levels of sub-subheads, the final level being **side heads**, which are run into the text, either beginning at the left margin or using a paragraph indentation.

BRAIN TICKLERS
Set # 15

Make a list of the heads in Chapter 2 of this book, indicating their level and how you can identify each level.

(Answers are on pages 163–164.)

Space

Space is a design element of a text, used partially to give pages of text a pleasing, uncluttered appearance that is easy to look at. It is also used to separate chapters, sections, and paragraphs of text. The separations reveal underlying organization and signal changes in content. In imaginative literary works (plays, fiction, and poetry), space may indicate pauses in the action and/or the passage of time. Space on the page may often indicate a pause in our reading of the text—a short "breather" to establish the change—whatever it is.

Punctuation

Punctuation tells us many things about how to use our voices when we read. One of the reasons it tells us so much is that it has three separate roles. On the one hand, punctuation is a device that we use to help us put back into text some of what we lose when speech gets put on paper—we use punctuation to signal pitch, pauses, stress, and breathing—the rhythm and intonation of the voice, also called prosody.

On the other hand, punctuation can tell us about syntax—the understanding of the rules of sentence formation—by separating parts of sentences (e.g., a dependent clause from an independent clause or marking the boundary between two independent clauses) to establish their relationship.

Punctuation is also used to convey semantic—or meaning—information. A grammatical comma, for example, doesn't convey meaning in the same way as a semantic comma. Without even looking at the content (the words), we can see the following kinds of meanings:

MEANINGS OF PUNCTUATION

The meaning	How it's indicated
parenthetical material	dashes, parentheses
a pause in time	ellipsis
omitted material	ellipsis
someone's words	quotation marks
someone quoting someone else	quotation marks within quotation marks
coordination	series of items separated by commas or semicolons
apposition (renaming)	set off by commas
interpolations or interjections	set off by commas
nonrestrictive material	set off by commas

Two of these conceptions of punctuation—syntactic (or grammatical) and prosodic—have actually fueled a "kommakrigen" or comma war in Denmark, where there is a battle raging between the old comma (a grammatical comma, the use of which is based on German rules of punctuation) and the New Comma, a prosodic comma introduced in 1996 and inserted in prose to indicate breaths in the natural rhythm of speech.

We don't have a war over punctuation here, but you will find that writers who are experts at their craft use punctuation with more attention and more skill than do writers who are less expert or new to the task. Paying careful attention when you read will allow you to use punctuation to identify prosodic, syntactic, and semantic pauses and convert them to what famous actor/director Constantin Stanislavski identifies as **logical pauses** (those that unite words into groups) and **psychological pauses** (the eloquent silence that can convey any number of meanings, depending on context). Then you can find the vocalization of a text that will prove the most meaningful in the context in which you will read it. Pauses are explored in more detail beginning on page 137.

Here's a brief survey of the kinds of punctuation and how they might guide your decisions about using your voice to make meaning.

End marks (periods, question marks, exclamation points) often indicate pitch shifts because we tend to raise pitch in questions and lower it toward the end of statements and may do either in exclamations, depending on the content. End marks also usually indicate a place to pause and to breathe, though if you were reading a series of short (one- or two-word) sentences, you would likely not breathe after each one.

Remember that a sentence is not a complete thought unless it also happens to be an utterance. Usually, a sentence is only a part of an utterance and, therefore, has important connections with the material that comes before and after. These connections will help guide you in knowing how you should connect the sentences.

HELPFUL HINT

If what you are reading is a script, a short story, or a novel, you must be aware of utterance on two levels: the entire text that you have (which could be hundreds of pages)—the writer's utterance—and an utterance within the world of the text, for example, a speech by one character in a play or a bit of dialogue by one character in a short story.

Pauses of various lengths *within* sentences are indicated by the following marks (from longest pause to shortest): ellipsis points, parentheses, dash, colon, semicolon, comma. (For long pauses *outside of* sentences, you'll find rows of dashes or asterisks, or white space on the page.) Each punctuation mark has specific uses.

- **Ellipsis points** may indicate three different things: an omission (for example, in a quotation or when a sentence trails off without being completed), a passage of time, or a pause longer than is indicated by a dash.

- **Parentheses** mark material that has the least possible connection to the rest of the text.
- The **em dash** shows a change in the construction of the sentence (its syntax), a turn of thought, or hesitancy.
- The **colon** says, in effect, *that is* or *for example* and is sometimes used in place of these words to introduce material. It is also used after the words *such as, namely, as follows,* or *for instance*. Sometimes a colon introduces a list; sometimes, a complete sentence.
- Even though the **semicolon**, like the comma, has the basic meaning of addition (and), it indicates a more significant break than a comma and a longer pause in reading. If one or more items in a series contain commas, semicolons are often used to separate the items to keep the meaning clear.
- The **comma** is the (almost) all-purpose, low-key punctuation mark to show the relationship between words, phrases, and clauses. The length of the pause depends on the particular function the comma is carrying out.

Many pauses are followed by a pitch shift to indicate to the listener that there's been a change.

Apostrophes signal **elision**, the omission of a syllable by dropping it or slurring it into the next syllable. (You saw examples of this on pages 108–109 to show dialect.) This is explicit information about how to voice the text.

Double quotation marks indicate that the words of a person or character other than the text's author, narrator, or speaker are being included, shifting us into characterization (our decisions about intonation when we see this will rest on how carefully we have been able to identify that person or character). They can also indicate irony by indicating a contrast between what is said and what is meant (e.g., He said he'd help me when he has some "spare" time—might be read as, He'll never make time to help me.).

Single quotation marks are used for quotations within quotations and may also be used to indicate irony (standing for *so-called*), calling for an increase in intensity, an introductory pause to gather attention, and a pitch shift.

The symbols called accent marks inform us about pronunciation. They may signal a particular sound (like the German umlaut ¨), tell us which syllable of a word to stress, or indicate that an ordinarily silent vowel should be pronounced. This last is the function of the grave accent (`) in English, which indicates that a syllable (often *–ed*) that is usually assimilated into (included in) the previous syllable is in this case pronounced as a separate syllable. Most of the time, this is found in older poetry to make a line fit the poetic meter.

BRAIN TICKLERS
Set # 16

1. Read each scenario. Choose the punctuated sentence that you think best answers the question. Explain the function of each punctuation mark (prosodic, syntactic, or semantic) and tell what the punctuation mark accomplishes.
   a. Several members of a committee have been uncooperative in planning an event. Arriving unprepared, they have taken up everybody's time going over material that should have been mastered previously. The leader of the meeting makes a comment. Which rendering gives the reader the best guide to demonstrate the leader's overwhelming frustration?
      i. Now that we've gone over that, can we get down to planning please?
      ii. Now that we've gone over that, can we get down to planning, please?
      iii. Now that we've gone over that, can we get down to planning . . . please!
   b. I have several aunts, but only one uncle. My aunt refers to her husband, whose given name is Henry, as Huck. I think my uncle is terrific. Which of the following conveys that information most clearly?
      i. My aunt, Susie, calls my uncle, Henry—the dear man!—"Huck."

      ii. My aunt Susie calls my uncle Henry the dear man Huck.

      iii. My aunt Susie calls my uncle Henry (the dear man) "Huck."

2. Read the following passages. Explain how orthography, typography, and punctuation convey meaning, and how you might translate this information into choices if you were to read each passage aloud.

   a. From *The Crisis* Number I by Thomas Paine, December 23, 1776:

These are the times that try men's souls: The summer soldier and the sunshine patriot will, in this crisis, shrink from the service of his country; but he that stands it NOW, deserves the love and thanks of man and woman. Tyranny, like hell, is not easily conquered; yet we have this consolation with us, that the harder the conflict, the more glorious the triumph. What we obtain too cheap, we esteem too lightly: 'Tis dearness only that gives every thing its value. Heaven knows how to put a proper price upon its goods; and it would be strange indeed, if so celestial an article as FREEDOM should not be highly rated. Britain, with an army to enforce her tyranny, has declared that she has a right (*not only to* TAX) but "to BIND us in ALL CASES WHATSOEVER," and if being *bound in that manner*, is not slavery, then is there not such a thing as slavery upon earth. Even the expression is impious, so unlimited a power can belong only to GOD.

   b. From "The Purloined Letter" by Edgar Allen Poe, 1845:
Note: The Prefect of the Parisian police, Monsieur G——, has come to visit detective C. Auguste Dupin and Dupin's friend, the narrator. His case is going badly.

At length I said,—

   "Well, but G——, what of the purloined letter? I presume you have at last made up your mind that there is no such thing as overreaching the Minister?"

   "Confound him, say I—yes; I made the re-examination, however, as Dupin suggested—but it was all labour lost, as I knew it would be."

   "How much was the reward offered, did you say?" asked Dupin.

   "Why, a very great deal—a very liberal reward—I don't like to say how much, precisely; but one thing I will say, that I wouldn't mind giving my individual cheque for fifty thousand francs to anyone who could obtain me that letter. The fact is, it is becoming of more and more importance every day; and the reward has been lately doubled. If it were trebled, however, I could do no more than I have done."

"Why, yes," said Dupin, drawlingly, between the whiffs of his meerschaum, "I really—think, G——, you have not exerted yourself—to the utmost in this matter. You might—do a little more, I think, eh?"

"How?—in what way?"

"Why—puff, puff—you might—puff, puff—employ counsel in the matter, eh?—puff, puff, puff. . . ."

"But," said the Prefect, a little discomposed, "I am perfectly willing to take advice, and to pay for it. I would really give fifty thousand francs to any who would aid me in the matter."

"In that case," replied Dupin, opening a drawer, and producing a cheque-book "you may as well fill me up a cheque for the amount mentioned. When you have signed it, I will hand you the letter."

I was astounded. The Prefect appeared absolutely thunder-stricken. For some minutes he remained speechless and motionless, looking incredulously at my friend with open mouth, and eyes that seemed starting from their sockets; then, apparently recovering himself in some measure, he seized a pen, and after several pauses and vacant stares, finally filled up and signed a cheque for fifty thousand francs, and handed it across the table to Dupin. The latter examined it carefully and deposited it in his pocket-book; then, unlocking an escritoire, took thence a letter and gave it to the Prefect. This functionary grasped it in a perfect agony of joy, opened it with a trembling hand, cast a rapid glance at its contents, and then scrambling and struggling to the door, rushed at length unceremoniously from the room and from the house, without having uttered a syllable since Dupin had requested him to fill up the cheque.

(Answers are on pages 164–165.)

Extra material (footnotes, appendices, glossaries, etc.)

As you are reading the body of a text, you may come to references that guide you to other parts of the book. Perhaps a super-script will direct you to a footnote or a parenthetical reference will direct you to the works cited page. Consider whether the thread of thought or argument will be strengthened or lost by an excursion to the material referenced when you are reading aloud.

Word order

Now we will turn our attention to the words themselves and what we can learn from them about how to use our voices in presenting a reading.

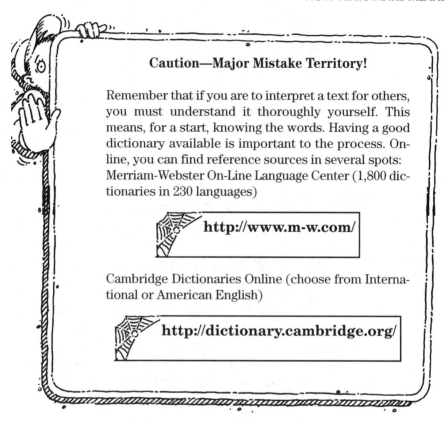

Caution—Major Mistake Territory!

Remember that if you are to interpret a text for others, you must understand it thoroughly yourself. This means, for a start, knowing the words. Having a good dictionary available is important to the process. On-line, you can find reference sources in several spots: Merriam-Webster On-Line Language Center (1,800 dictionaries in 230 languages)

http://www.m-w.com/

Cambridge Dictionaries Online (choose from International or American English)

http://dictionary.cambridge.org/

Word order, or **syntax**, serves many functions. For one thing, it helps bring important words to our attention. Writers may highlight words by placing them at the beginning and end of a sentence, paragraph, or text. In literary works, focusing on word placement can help us identify theme and overall meaning.

Rhetorical devices, called **tropes**, work with word placement and repetition of words to highlight meaning by helping us focus on the most important words and phrases in particular configurations. As readers conveying texts, we need to recognize when writers are using such devices so that we can bring them to the listener's attention. For more information about tropes, check out *A Handlist of Rhetorical Terms* by Richard A. Lanham.

BREAKING THE RULES OF MEANING MAKING

Sometimes the rules of meaning making that we usually use to figure out how to understand words don't apply. We are going to discuss three particular cases: figurative language, idioms, and irony.

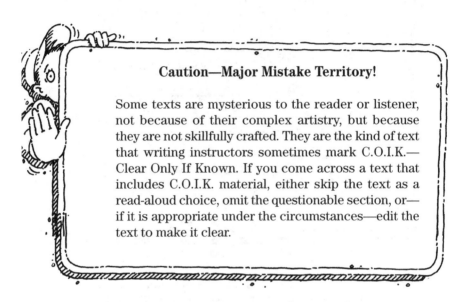

Caution—Major Mistake Territory!

Some texts are mysterious to the reader or listener, not because of their complex artistry, but because they are not skillfully crafted. They are the kind of text that writing instructors sometimes mark C.O.I.K.— Clear Only If Known. If you come across a text that includes C.O.I.K. material, either skip the text as a read-aloud choice, omit the questionable section, or— if it is appropriate under the circumstances—edit the text to make it clear.

Figurative language

Figures of speech are groups of words that cannot be understood literally. They include the following:

- A **simile** is a comparison using words such as *like*, *as*, or *as if*.
  To understand the simile, we must find the likeness. Many similes have become clichés (*as pretty as a picture*; *as light as a feather*), which makes them ineffective in communication, except, perhaps, to communicate that a character's thinking is commonplace or hackneyed. On the other hand, a simile that is too obscure in its point of comparison may be open to misinterpretation.
- A **metaphor** compares two things that are in fact different (but we must be able to figure out how they are alike).

- **Personification** is a metaphorical figure in which human characteristics are attributed to animals or inanimate objects.
- **Hyperbole** is overstatement, exaggeration for effect.
- **Meiosis** is understatement for effect. It is the opposite of hyperbole and may have the effect of praising or belittling. Meiosis includes **euphemism**, the substitution of a neutral or inoffensive phrase for one that is strong or offensive. I would be intending praise if I said, "Hey, this is not a bad party"—I'd actually mean "This is a *great* party." But Oscar Wilde was certainly intending to belittle when he said about fox hunting: "The English country gentleman galloping after a fox—the unspeakable in full pursuit of the uneatable."

Idioms

Idioms are like metaphors in that you cannot infer the meaning from the literal meaning of the individual words alone. Unlike metaphors, they are groups of words that have acquired set meanings—so set that you can look them up in the dictionary. Some linguists think that idioms started as metaphors and then became set in stone (and there's an idiom). Idioms may become clichés through overuse.

SAMPLE IDIOMS

Idiom	Meaning
a nine days' wonder	a matter creating short-lived but intense interest
apple pie order	careful neatness
got up on the wrong side of bed	in a bad mood
to have on the carpet	to interrogate, reprimand, and punish
to know the ropes	to be knowledgeable and adept
wrote the book on x	knows everything there is to know about x

Clearly, you need to know the meaning of idioms in order to be able to interpret them to your listeners.

Irony

Irony comes from a Greek word meaning someone who hides under a false appearance. When irony is used, things appear different, even the opposite, of what they really are; unexpected events happen; what people say is not what they mean. Authors use irony to create interest, surprise, or an understanding with their readers that the characters do not share. There are three types of irony.

Verbal irony is irony in the use of language. Verbal irony means that what is said is different from or the opposite of what is meant. A difference between tone of voice and the content of what is said is one kind of verbal irony.

In dramatic irony, there is knowledge that the narrator makes available to the reader, but the characters are unaware of it.

Situational irony can occur from the point of view of either a character or the reader. It describes a situation when something that is expected with a great deal of certainty doesn't happen (this can be from either point of view) or when something that is intended fails to materialize (this is only possible from a character's point of view, except in Choose–Your–Own Adventures or other books in which the reader participates by making a choice).

BRAIN TICKLERS
Set # 17

Read this excerpt from Benjamin Franklin's satirical essay, "RULES by which a Great Empire may be Reduced to a Small One: Presented to a Late Minister, when He Entered Upon His Administration" (from *The Public Advertiser*, September 8, 1773).

Note the use Franklin makes of typography, orthography, punctuation, figurative language, idioms, irony, and any other patterns you see. Speak the excerpt aloud so as to give it the most meaning.

An ancient Sage valued himself upon this, that tho' he could not fiddle, he knew how to make a *great City of a little one*. The Science that I, a modern Simpleton, am about to communicate is the very reverse.

I address myself to all Ministers who have the Management of extensive Dominions, which from their very Greatness are become troublesome to govern, because the Multiplicity of their Affairs leaves no Time for *fiddling*.

I. In the first Place, Gentlemen, you are to consider, that a great Empire, like a great Cake, is most easily diminished at the Edges. Turn your Attention therefore first to your remotest Provinces; that as you get rid of them, the next may follow in Order.

II. That the Possibility of this Separation may always exist, take special Care the Provinces are never incorporated with the Mother Country, that they *do not enjoy the same common Rights*, the same *Privileges in Commerce*, and that they are governed by *severer* Laws, all of *your enacting*, without allowing them any Share in the Choice of the Legislators. By carefully making and preserving such Distinctions, you will (to keep to my Simile of the Cake) act like a wise Gingerbread Baker, who, to facilitate a Division, cuts his Dough half through in those Places, where, when bak'd, he would have it *broken to Pieces.*

III. These remote Provinces have perhaps been acquired, purchas'd, or conquer'd, at the *sole Expence* of the Settlers or their Ancestors, without the Aid of the Mother Country. If this should happen to increase her *Strength* by their growing Numbers ready to join in her Wars, her *Commerce* by their growing Demand for her Manufactures, or her *Naval Power* by greater Employment for her Ships and Seamen, they may probably suppose some Merit in this, and that it entitles them to some Favour; you are therefore to forget it all, or resent it as if they had done you Injury. If they happen to be zealous Whigs, Friends of Liberty, nurtur'd in Revolution Principles, *remember all that to their Prejudice*, and contrive to punish it: For such Principles, after a Revolution is thoroughly established, are of *no more Use*, they are even *odious* and *abominable*.

IV. However peaceably your Colonies have submitted to your Government, shewn their Affection to your Interest, and patiently borne their Grievances, you are to *suppose* them always inclined to revolt, and treat them accordingly. Quarter Troops among them, who by their Insolence may *provoke* the rising of Mobs, and by their Bullets and Bayonets *suppress* them. By this Means, like the Husband who uses his Wife ill *from Suspicion,* you may in Time convert your *Suspicions* into *Realities.*

(Answers are on pages 165–166.)

MAKING DECISIONS ABOUT STRESSES AND PAUSES

So far in this chapter, we've mentioned stresses and pauses a number of times, but primarily in terms of the signals we find in the text. Now we're going to round off this section by looking at them in terms of your decision-making process.

Using stress

Recall that **stress** is a little extra oomph that the voice gives to words to call the listener's attention to them. We do this to help listeners make connections and follow the flow of ideas. In prose, we often stress:

- Important words like the subject and the predicate.
- Words that the writer has privileged by putting them first or last in a phrase, clause, sentence, or paragraph, or repeating them, particularly in a rhetorical trope.
- Words that link sentences, like a noun that will be referred back to by a pronoun in the next sentence.
- Words that provide transitions, like conjunctions.
- Words that convey the particular meaning we choose to give to a sentence that might be construed in multiple ways, in other words, to reveal the subtext (see page 6). H. Wesley Balk, author of *Performing Power: A New Approach for the Singer-Actor* (University of Minnesota Press, 1986), explains this principle (p. 113) in a chart that explores possible ways to speak the line "I love you."

MEANINGS OF "I LOVE YOU"

How it's said	What it means
I love you.	Unstressed, the basic verbal meaning is that the speaker has a deep feeling about the person being addressed.

Continued

How it's said   **What it means**

<u>I</u> love you.   Even if someone else doesn't.

I <u>love</u> you.   As opposed to simply loving you in the
ordinary sense of that word.

I love <u>you</u>.   I love you <u>too</u>, responding to a person who has
just said, "I love you."

<u>I</u> love <u>you</u>.   But I don't think <u>you</u> love <u>me</u>.

I <u>love</u> you.   And someone else just likes you.

To which we might add

<u>I</u> . . . <u>love</u>   Moment of revelation—I didn't realize it until
. . . <u>you</u>.   just now.

- Words that indicate what the writer is doing. So, we would
  stress words that indicate genre (*Once upon a time*, there
  was a . . .), task (How do the newest palm organizers *compare*?), or purpose (*act* now to . . .).

You know many of the genre words. The purpose words (as in the example) are often directed to the audience (in direct address). We are now going to focus on identifying words that relate to the task the writer is carrying out.

Each of the six tasks can express one or more relationships. Spotting the relationship can often lead to identifying the task. Use this chart to help you.

TASKS AND THE RELATIONSHIPS THEY CAN EXPRESS

Task/Graphic Organizer	Relationship
Compare/Contrast (Type 1)	Differences or Opposition
Compare/Contrast (Type 2)	Similarities
Define (Type 1)	Thing and its Change over Time
Define (Type 2)	Thing and its Function(s)
Define (Type 3)	Thing and its Components/ Examples of It
Define (Type 4)	Thing and its Attributes or Description
Define (Type 5)	Thing and its (necessary) Associations
Define (Type 6)	Thing and its Meaning
Define (Type 7)	Thing and its Purpose(s)
Define (Type 8)	Thing and its Value/Thing Measured by Criteria
Define (Type 9)	Thing and its Environment
List	Conglomeration
Argue (Type 1)	Hypothesis
Argue (Type 2)	Problem & Solution/ Resolution/Amelioration
Argue (Type 3)	Proposition/Support or Statement/Proof
Argue (Type 4)	Question and Answer

| Sequence (Type 1) | Cause/Effect |
| Sequence (Type 2) | Series of Events in Time |

| Classify (Type 1) | Subordination |

Once you identify the task, refer to the following chart to identify words that have a key function in helping the listener construct a meaningful understanding.

TASK/KEY WORDS AND PHRASES

Task

Key words and phrases

Compare/contrast	**Compare**	**Contrast**
	alike	although
	as well as	at the same time
	despite	but
	equally important	conversely
	in the same way	differ
	like	different from (than)
	likewise	however
	regardless	instead
	resemble	nevertheless
	similar to	on the contrary
	similarly	on the one hand
		on the other hand
		still
		though
		whereas
		while
		yet
Define	a kind of	characteristic
	attribute	concept
	category	connect
	connote	made up of
	contains	means

Continued

131

Task	Key words and phrases

cycle	means that
defined	near
denote	part
e.g.	part of
example	property
far	senses
feature	sight
feel	smell
for example	sort of
for instance	sound
function	specifically
hear	such as
in particular	system
includes	taste
is	that is
is called	touch
is named	type of
is referred to as	which is
link	whole

List

also	furthermore
and	in addition
another	including
as well as	moreover
besides	too

Argue

above all	difficulty
accept	effects
although	either . . . or
because	even though
causes	fact
claim	for example
consequences	for this reason
cure	granted that
data	hence
hypothesis	positive
if	premise

Continued

Task

Key words and phrases

if . . . then	problem
in conclusion	proof
in spite of	proposition
indeed	prove
indicate	quote
inference	rather than
instead of	reason
limitation	so that
more important	solution
negative	suggest
neither . . . nor	support
nevertheless	then
notwithstanding	theory
of course	therefore
otherwise	thesis
persuade	unless

Sequence

accordingly	factors
action	finally
after	first, second,
afterwards	third, . . .
and they lived	follow
happily ever	for this reason
after	goal
attempt	history
because	if . . . then
before	incident
cause	last
climax	later
consequently	meanwhile
(dates)	motivation
denouement	nevertheless
earlier	next
effect	now
event	once upon a time
outcome	stages
presently	steps

Continued

133

Task	Key words and phrases	
	previously	subsequently
	prior	the end
	resolution	then
	result	therefore
	reversal	thus
	since	time
	situation	to begin with
	so that	ultimately
	soon	
Classify	assorted	mixed
	assortment	nature
	bracket	order
	brand	phylum
	breed	property
	category	quality
	characteristics	race
	criteria	rank
	description	section
	division	sort
	family	species
	feature	standard
	genre	stock
	genus	strain
	grade	style
	group	subdivision
	heterogeneous	subset
	homogenous	tier
	hybrid	trait
	kind	type
	manner	variety

Beyond task

To understand more clearly the import of the particular words in the particular sentence you are trying to convey (which is determined by the **context** of the sentence), questions like these may prove helpful:

- What's already understood by all parties?
- What information is new?
- Of the new information, what is most crucial?
- How does the new information link to what's known?
- What relationships among thoughts, ideas, and concepts are being conveyed?
- What is the subtext?

Also consider whether you should stress more than one word, and how you might combine stress with other vocal techniques (pausing, pitch change, etc.) to create the effects you seek. And always consider the sentence in the context of the entire utterance.

Look at how the context shifts in this dialogue, necessitating a change in which words are stressed in the answers to the questions:

K: Is the money under the stove?

Q: No, it's under the *dresser*.

K: I said, "Is the money under the stove?"

Q: No, the *crown jewels* are under the *stove*; the *money* is under the *dresser*.

K: Did you say the money is on the dresser?

Q: No, the money is not *on* the dresser; the money is *under* the dresser.

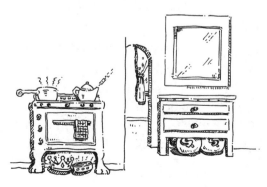

The absolutely most essential word in the last sentence is the preposition *under*. We can assume that (finally) in the context in which the last utterance was made, *money* and *dresser* were already understood by both parties. The essential information that was not yet shared between them was the exact relationship of the money to the dresser, which is conveyed by the preposition *under*.

The kind of stress in this final sentence is called **contrastive stress**: two (or more) elements are being set against each other, and so each receives vocal stress. **Additive stress** refers to items that are being compared.

BRAIN TICKLERS
Set # 18

Identify the words that should be stressed in each sentence. Find a way to say each of these sentences so that the meaning is clear. The last one is a real challenge!

1. The turnips were not on the table, but in the bathtub.
2. The turnips were not stacked on the table, but piled in the bathtub.
3. The turnips were both piled in the bathtub and stashed in the linen cupboard.
4. The chickens were neither white nor brown.
5. The chickens were neither white nor brown, but a delicate shade of lavender.
6. "In the progress of politics, as in the common occurrences of life, we are not only apt to forget the ground we have traveled over, but frequently neglect to gather up experience as we go." *The Crisis* Number III, Thomas Paine.
7. "Those who expect to reap the blessings of freedom, must, like men, undergo the fatigues of supporting it." *The Crisis* Number IV, Thomas Paine

8. "There is a dignity in the warm passions of a whig, which is never to be found in the cold malice of a tory." *The Crisis Number VI*, Thomas Paine

9. "It is not a little remarkable that in every case reported by ancient history in which government has been established with deliberation and consent, the task of framing it has not been committed to an assembly of men, but has been performed by some individual citizen of preeminent wisdom and approved integrity." *Federalist Paper No. 38*, Madison

10. I didn't say to meet at the green house: I said, "Meet me at the greenhouse!"

(Answers are on pages 166–167.)

Using pauses

Constantin Stanislavski, in his work *Building a Character*, emphasizes the importance of the pause in speech by comparing two sentences in which the placement of the pause means mercy or exile:

> Pardon—impossible send to Siberia.
> Pardon impossible—send to Siberia.

Of course, not every pause you use will approach this example in importance, but it is a good idea to note the pauses suggested by prosody, syntax, and semantics (the three kinds of pauses indicated by punctuation) and to consider how exactly you will convey them as logical or psychological pauses. Ask yourself these questions:

- How long will I pause?
- What do I mean to convey by the pause—hesitation, fear, anger, frustration, desire that someone else speak first, a pause for a character to get thoughts straight, an inability to speak due to an overwhelming flood of emotion, or something else?
- I will not be speaking, but what will I be doing? Will I look up at my listeners? Will I breathe during the pause? Will I gesture? Will I move?
- H. Wesley Balk in *Performing Power: A New Approach for the Singer-Actor* gives a list of possible meanings for what he refers to as the **tactical pause**: "A pause can say 'I don't like what I'm going to say' or 'I *relish* what I am going to say,' or 'Listen very carefully to what I say next,' or 'Did you hear what I just said? I'm going to give you time to assimilate it,' or 'I just had an idea that stopped my previous train of thought and launched me on a new one.' The most important message, however, is the one that accompanies all the preceding examples: 'I haven't finished. Continue to pay attention, in fact pay *closer* attention!'" (p. 132).

PREPARING TO READ ALOUD

If you are going to have an opportunity to read aloud and you have a chance to prepare, then this is the place for you to pick up the pointers and tips to help you through the process. If you're anticipating having to read on the spot with no preparation, you'll find helpful hints further along, beginning on page 241.

Text and context

You might think that the text is the crucial element of the reading experience. But there are three other essential parts of the reading situation: you, your listener or listeners, and the situation or context. Let's look at each in turn.

So here you are, preparing to read aloud. How does the person you are enter into the situation? Well first, you're a person with a particular **learning style**, a particular **performance mode** (see page 27), and particular **kinds of intelligence** (see page 28). You have certain **skills**, **gifts**, and **talents**—perhaps some of these you've had the opportunity to develop to a certain extent—and particular **interests**. You have an accumulation of **knowledge about texts and speech genres**, as well as more or less **prior knowledge about the content area** that is covered in whatever text you will be reading aloud. You may or may not look forward with a **level of enthusiasm** to the reading aloud situation and you may have had great or uncomfortable **past experiences**. And **whatever is going on in your life** at the particular moment of reading has its effect as well.

Except that we are talking about mode of *response* to performance rather than performing mode, the categories for your listener or listeners are the same as for you. But add in that if you have multiple listeners, you have to try to address the whole range of their interests, modes, and abilities at once. This can be especially difficult if you don't know too much about your audience.

Now add in the situation. The situation context includes the **function** and **purpose** of the reading (for the listeners, for the reader, and for the sponsoring organization if there is one), the **setting**, the **occasion**, the **available resources**, the **limitations**, and the **outside influences**. Here are some questions to help you think through the situation. (Note that this list is not definitive; you may think of other questions.)

What function does this reading have for the listeners?

first hearing of a text they're going to be tested on?

story hour?

public lecture that they choose to hear?

fun with an older sibling?

What function does this reading have for you?

lesson for a class in public speaking?

volunteer work for a local nursing home?

public lecture that you choose to deliver?

fun with a younger sibling?

What is the purpose of this reading event—from your point of view and from the listeners' point of view? Do your ideas about purpose match or complement each other?

What are the parameters of the setting?

classroom? office? home? theatre? something else?

How many listeners will there be?

Did you volunteer, were you invited, is this part of a job, or is this a class obligation?

Will you have time to prepare, or will you have to read "cold"?

Are there other readers besides yourself?

Is this just you and a text, or are there props, costumes, make-up, audiovisual aides, or other materials to enhance your performance?

What is the occasion of the reading?

Is it connected to a celebration or event?

Is it a regular meeting of a group (a class, a library reading group, a lecture series, etc.)?

Is there a series of readings being done on one day?

Are there other, related presentations going on?

What important events or happenings are influencing—or impinging on—the situation: school, home, business, or world events?

Thinking more about your listeners

You may remember some of the points made when we talked about orality and literacy in terms of conversation (see page 59). As a listener instead of a reader, you can't look back to see what happened earlier—you have to rely on your memory. As a listener, it's easier to think about concrete material than abstract material. As a listener, it's difficult to deal with a lot of complexity. Repetition and mnemonics help with recall. But to do a really fine job of preparing for and delivering an aural message, you need to know how it is processed.

What happens when you hear speech

On page 91, I listed the steps in the reading process—how we process black marks on the white page in order to understand and integrate the meaning of a text. When words are heard, things are a little different.

A spoken utterance is first received by the listener as a semi-continuous acoustic signal with pauses only when the speaker pauses. Did you ever stop to think that sound doesn't come to us divided into words and phrases? Our first task as listeners is the task of **segmentation**. As listeners, we must simultaneously analyze the speech signal into **phonemes** (sounds), **morphemes** (meaning units), words, phrases, sentences, units of discourse (like tasks), and utterances (complete concepts or ideas). We search our mental **lexicon** (dictionary) for **phonological strings** (groups of sounds) that match what we've heard, pre-analyzed into our best guess at word units. When we find a match, this brings up the **semantics** (meaning) of the word unit we've identified. We then use stress and intonation, as well as relative loudness, pitch, and duration of syllables to help guide us in understanding the **syntactic structure** (word order) of the utterance. And this amazingly complex process is so speedy and automatic that we can do all this and prepare our own response at the same time!

What if we don't find a match for one or more phonological strings? Then we can try to use other information to refine our guess (e.g., infer the word from context); we can skip it, if it doesn't seem too important to the meaning; or we can ask the speaker for assistance in interpreting.

What if the semantic and syntactic information doesn't combine into an interpretable sentence? As suggested above, we refine our guess using additional information, decide that we can do without the particular piece of the message, or ask for help.

We can use our awareness of this complex process to remind ourselves to be thoughtful readers.

Choosing a text

So, in choosing a text, should we have the opportunity, we have these things to keep in mind: the text itself, the reader, the listener, the context, and the nature of listening and orality. Life could be really easy: you could offer to read to your little sister, and she could blurt out, "I want *Don't Tell Me a Ghost Story!*" which just happens to be a book you read over and over as a child and would love to read to her because it has really good spooky ghost noises and a ghost named Mooooooky Blooooooky in it. In case life doesn't turn out to be so simple, follow along here for some solid guidelines.

Texts have different aims, and so we cannot make a general rule for choosing them except this: whatever they are trying to do, they should do well (unless our purpose in reading is to demonstrate their failure). We expect different excellencies from a story than from a letter; we hope for different enjoyment from a well-conceived essay than from a play.

Literary critic and researcher Louise Rosenblatt noted that a reader approaches a text along a continuum, with efferent reading at one extreme and/or aesthetic reading at the other. **Efferent reading** focuses on the *information* to be acquired, while **aesthetic reading** focuses on the *reader's experience* during the reading event. Rosenblatt says that aesthetic reading is the special mark of the literary work of art because it is lived through by the reader.

Aesthetic texts

Henry David Thoreau says in *Walden*, "Could a greater miracle take place than for us to look through each other's eyes for an instant?" Books that have a story structure—fiction, autobiography, travelogues, history, and so on—can give us that view, and these are all books that we as readers, or listeners, experience aesthetically.

What is it that allows aesthetic experience to happen? It is the result of a combination of factors, one of the most important being that the text is so unified and coherent that nothing within the text knocks you outside the world of the story. In talking about the "willing suspension of disbelief"—the name that poet Samuel Taylor Coleridge gave to what we do when we temporarily give up the world of reality and enter the world of aesthetic experience—J. R. R. Tolkien says in his essay "Tree and Leaf," ". . . the story-maker . . . makes a Secondary World which your mind can enter. Inside it, what he relates is 'true': it accords with the laws of that world. You therefore believe it, while you are, as it were, inside. The moment disbelief arises, the spell is broken; the magic, or rather art, has failed. You are then out in the Primary [real] World again, looking at the little abortive Secondary World from outside." So if you find a text in which

- the dialogue is unbelievable,
- the diction is inconsistent,
- the characterization is weak,

- the characters' motivations don't seem to fit,
- the plot is convoluted or wildly improbable, or
- the attitudes seem inappropriate to the characters,

put it aside and search for something with more coherence.

Aesthetic experience also depends on the presentation. Edgar Allen Poe, in his essay "Twice-Told Tales," says that aesthetic experience happens when one experiences "totality." But totality is easily missed if "worldly interests, intervening during the pauses of perusal, modify, counteract and annul the impressions intended." So you want to be able to read uninterrupted so your listeners experience the entire utterance without pause. And— thinking about the facts we know about listening, processing, and recall—this means that you may want to choose a text with an appropriate level of vocabulary and complexity, and a memorable storyline so that your audience will not feel the need to break the spell of totality by interjecting questions.

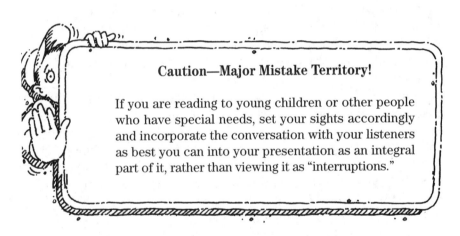

Caution—Major Mistake Territory!

If you are reading to young children or other people who have special needs, set your sights accordingly and incorporate the conversation with your listeners as best you can into your presentation as an integral part of it, rather than viewing it as "interruptions."

Literature, being art, is also about fulfilling and denying expectations, of leading the reader/listener on a chase until a satisfying (though not necessarily happy) ending is reached. To this end look for:

- a plot that is suspenseful and interesting
- themes that resonate with what you know of life
- characters that are admirable or at least fascinating
- vivid description that evokes your imagination
- valuable insights and understandings that enrich your life

- a sense of emotional expansion from having lived through the story

Efferent texts

Unlike an aesthetic text, an efferent text should be as pre-dictable as possible: every connection should be clear, and every piece of information and its relation to the whole, evident. Whereas an aesthetic piece may hope to thrill you by starting *in medias res* (in the middle of things), a well-written efferent piece should "begin at the beginning . . . and go on till [it] come[s] to the end: then stop," as the White King advised Alice.

In talking about textbook design in 1984 ("Content Area Textbooks" in *Learning to Read in American Schools: Basal Readers and Content Texts*, Lawrence Erlbaum Associates, Publishers, 1984), researchers Bonnie B. Armbruster and Thomas H. Anderson defined a considerate text as one "designed to enable the reader to gather appropriate information with minimal cognitive effort." Since all efferent texts are designed to transmit information, I propose that we can use Armbruster and Anderson's four evaluative categories—structure, coherence, unity, and audience appropriateness—to help us judge all texts that we listen to for information.

Structure

Armbruster and Anderson say that **the topic, purpose, and structure of the text should be readily apparent from the headings and/or topic sentences.** Skip the text for a moment, and read through the headings of the section of text you are considering using. Then read through only the first sentence of each paragraph. Can you follow along in these ways? If so, you have a well-structured text. What Armbruster and Anderson say about structure for readers is ever so much more true for listeners, who have, in many cases, no visual cues to support their memories, who cannot "look back."

Coherence

Coherence means holding together. It means that **connections in the text should be clear—both connections between and among ideas and events mentioned in the text, and connections between and among elements of the text (i.e., words, phrases, clauses, sentences).** This implies that relationships between and among ideas and events should be explicitly stated. References from one part of the text to another (e.g., pronoun references and quantifiers like *few, some, many*) should be clear. Sequences of events should move through time in one direction only.

Does the text include any portions that have the six tasks we noted: compare and contrast, define, list, argue, sequence, and classify (see the chart on pages 130–131)? If so, you can check for the key words noted on pages 131–134. Does the text use these words to make connections?

Unity

Armbruster and Anderson use *unity* to mean singularity of purpose. Unity includes whatever the writer intends to do; in Bakhtin's terms, **the text should be an utterance—no more, no less. In other words, the text should be finalized.** This can be the case only if every idea in the text contributes to the purpose—material that is ancillary to the main purpose should appear in footnotes, appendices, sidebars, or charts, not within the main body of the work. Although they do not mention it, another failure of unity would be the omission of material that is essential to the complete rendering of the writer's purpose.

Audience appropriateness

We've already talked a bit about listener characteristics such as response mode and intelligence (page 139). Armbruster and Anderson speak specifically only of the **text matching the reader's (read listener's) knowledge base**. The knowledge base includes prior knowledge about speech genres that allows the reader to predict the text structure, as well as prior knowledge about the content area. If it is necessary to introduce technical terms or other difficult vocabulary, the terms should be defined clearly upon first usage, and their meanings repeated, if it seems necessary. Any use of language that cannot be literally construed—irony, idioms, or rhetorical figures—should be carefully considered in terms of the audience. Check analogies for clarity, too.

The amount of complexity is also a consideration. Although they raise this issue in terms of unity, Armbruster and Anderson's citation of a study by G. A. Miller in *Psychological Review* (1956), which found that short-term memory can hold only about five to nine items at one time, seems more pertinent here. Armbruster and Anderson suggest that poor and beginning readers would have more difficulty than average readers with complex text (perhaps they'd remember fewer than five items). It is not difficult to believe that inexperienced listeners or those listening to a second language might also have difficulty.

Other considerations

Also think about the following factors:

- How much time do you have to make your presentation? Is the piece a good match or will you have to cut or excerpt it? Do you have the skill and time to do so?
- Can the text you are thinking about stand on its own? Would it work with a short introduction? Or is it too complicated to use in the given time?
- Would doing an excellent job of preparation require a lot of research on your part? Do you have the time and resources to complete such research?

Pre-reading a text

It stands to reason that all those text cues that we talked about on pages 108–134 help you much more if you identify and think about them *before* you actually start reading to your audience. It's much harder to catch all the clues on the fly than it is to pick them up during a slow, thoughtful preparation time. Writer Vladimir Nabokov goes so far as to say in his lecture on "Good Readers and Good Writers," "one cannot *read* a book: one can only reread it. . . . [W]e must have time to acquaint ourselves with it. We have no physical organ . . . that takes in the whole picture . . . [until] a second, or third, or fourth reading." When we reconsider the complexity of the task of reading (see page 91), this point makes sense.

And how do you pre-read? The philosopher Friedrich Nietzsche would answer, slowly. He says, in his preface to "Daybreak," "read slowly, deeply, looking cautiously before and aft, with reservations, with doors left open, with delicate eyes and fingers." This kind of thoughtful reading will help you find the clues and the patterns that will lead to the most rewarding reading experience. Here are some steps you can take:

Step 1: Identify the speech genre of a piece of text. Use the clues provided by its structure, style, content, conception of audience, and purpose. (For more detailed information on some major speech genres, see pages 95–105.)

Step 2: Go through the text and identify the tasks the writer carries out: compare and contrast, define, list, argue, sequence, and classify (see page 93). Jot notes in the margin. (If the text doesn't belong to you, and you are doing a school assignment, you may be able to get permission to make a copy.)

Step 3: Go through the text and identify the writer's purpose(s) (see pages 93–94).

Step 4: Now, as closely as possible, identify the writer's audience.

You should now have a good, general idea about what kind of a text you have before you.

Caution—Major Mistake Territory!

Don't think you can remember everything you find out about a text! Don't even try! Marking a text is an excellent way to maintain a record of your discoveries and your plans. In fact, marking a text is something you should do whenever possible because it's a good way to make a book your own. You can not only respond to the writer, narrator, speaker, and/or characters but also give yourself helpful reminders, collate information, and record your reactions to the unfolding of the plot. Here are some helpful hints on how reading with a pen or pencil can add depth to your experience.

Book as conversation

By definition, when you read a book, you're experiencing another person—the writer—who has something to say. With pen in hand, you can speak back. Questions, comments, evaluations, even arguments are fair game. Some comments you might want to use are

- Yes/No
- !!!!! (as many as you need)
- TAT ("think about this")—for points that need pondering
- WM? ("what [does this] mean?")—for points that need clarification

Or perhaps you've already developed some methods of your own.

Memory aids

If this text is important to you, you know that you're going to want to find things again. Using underlining and margin notes can help. Here are some ideas.

- Title untitled chapters with a name that will help you recall the contents.
- On the inside front cover or first page, list items you need to find again: important quotations, appearance of symbols, page numbers of significant events or information.
- Invent a system to record the occurrence of repetition, symbols, connections, themes, and other important details such as key words or important quotations in the margin.

Links/connections

As already indicated, noting places in which repetition ties one part of a book to another is important. But beyond that, sometimes a book will call up a link to another source—a reference or allusion will be known to you; a thought or quotation will connect to something someone else said or wrote in another book or medium. Write it in the margin. You may find the connection valuable later.

Reading instructions

Remember all those ways the text makes meaning? Marking the text is the way to call them out for yourself. You can develop a system to mark stresses, pauses, pitch shifts, changes in tone, use of character voices, and so on.

Flag it

Self-stick flags can be really helpful. One thing you may wish to do is mark each page that begins a chapter with a numbered flag. This makes locating information much quicker than thumbing through every time. You can color-code different topics to make your task easier.

Reading some important speech genres

Here are some guidelines for approaching the interpretation of nine different major speech genres: news stories, editorials, feature pieces, sports stories, reports, personal essays, stories or fiction, scripts, and poetry.

Newspaper articles

There are several specific subgenres within the category of newspaper articles. News stories are attempts at objective writing. They are front-loaded—that is, they attempt to answer the Five Ws and an H questions—Who? What? Where? When? Why? and How?—in the very first paragraph, so that readers might gather the gist of the day's news by reading the headline and first paragraph only of each of the front-page stories. There is little to "interpret" in reading a news story. Clarity and pacing to make sure that the bulk of information at the front is not overwhelming is important. There is no characterization (some news stories don't even have a byline identifying who wrote them—they simply are credited to a news wire service), and the use of intonation to show feeling is not appropriate when reading a news story as a news story.

Editorials are persuasive pieces. Some are unattributed and are just "the voice of the paper," while others come from established editorial writers who are known for their particular views, or even for their particular biases. Feature pieces may have some of the same topics as make the news section, but with a twist. Here there is humor, intrigue, passion. Both editorials and feature stories may be written from either the third-person or first-person point of view, but neither attempts to be objective. In each, it's important to identify the speaker, and to stick to the facts—this is not a character you're making up; this is a real, live human being. If you have the opportunity, you can read other articles or editorials by the same writer to expand your understanding of him or her.

For an editorial writer, you want to identify his or her values and perspective. For a feature writer, you want to figure out how to make the most of this "light touch" on the news by identifying the twist the writer takes. Does the story make the news into a feature by using the grotesque, humor, the unusual, local interest, an emotional appeal, or some other approach? Where's the excitement and drama in the piece? How can you best convey that with your voice?

Many sports stories appeal to very narrow audiences, although you may find some that deal with larger issues and so broaden their appeal. But a story about a particular game, no matter how well written, colorful, and exciting the prose, is likely to have limited interest beyond the folks who follow the sport or maybe, depending on the level of play, the particular teams involved in the competition. Reading a sports story well requires knowing the jargon. You must know the idioms and what they mean to give them appropriate intonation, and you need to know how to say the abbreviations. For example:

NCAA (National Collegiate Athletic Conference)
can be either N-C-double A or N-C-A-A
but
NESCAC (New England Small College Athletic Conference)
is /NES-kack/ not N-E-S-C-A-C

You can check with a local newspaper sports room for assistance.

Essays

You may find yourself reading aloud two distinctly different types of essays. The first is a factual, third-person, objectively written essay, which might, in some circumstances, be called a report. In this type of essay, the persona of the writer is usually somewhat concealed. You are not called upon, in this case, to develop characterization or a well-defined voice for the narrator. Your role here is to transmit, as clearly as possible, the information that is within the text, whether it is meant to inform, define, or explain.

The factual essay's appeal will usually depend on its topic, unless—which sometimes happens—the writer uses a microcosm to draw conclusions about the world at large in the end. In either case, if you are choosing material for an older audience, a good essay, even if it's on a topic in which they previously had no interest, may draw them in. In choosing material for a young audience, you may have to think carefully to find a topic that will hold their attention.

Personal essays are always written in the first person. Though the content may be focused on a very narrow field about which the writer has personal knowledge, the theme of a personal essay is usually some universal theme that expands the view from this field to life in general.

Here are some essayists whose work you may want to read.

Maya Angelou	Russell Baker	Sandra Cisneros
Annie Dillard	Ralph Waldo Emerson	Benjamin Franklin
John Hersey	Jamaica Kincaid	Maxine Hong Kingston
William Least Heat Moon	C. S. Lewis	George Orwell
Thomas Paine	Walker Percy	Lewis Thomas
Henry David Thoreau	James Thurber	John Updike
E. B. White	Richard Wright	

BRAIN TICKLERS
Set # 19

Find a story from a newspaper or an essay that you think would make good material for reading aloud in some context and do the following for it:

1. Define the context.
2. Pre-read the text using the four steps on page 148.
3. Mark the text.
4. Read the text aloud, pretending to be in front of an audience.

(Answers are on page 167.)

Stories/Fiction

"My task," said writer Joseph Conrad, in the introduction to *The Nigger of the 'Narcissus': A Tale of the Sea*, "which I am trying to achieve is, by the power of the written word, to make you hear, to make you feel—it is, before all, to make you *see*. That, and no more, and it is *everything*." When you read a story to listeners, don't think of yourself as just speaking words: think of yourself, as Thoreau said, as allowing your listeners to look through another's eyes for an instant.

Imaging during reading aloud is known to unify comprehension. We may well imagine that the same happens if we use our imaginations to picture a story that we *hear*. So when you look for stories, look for stories with which you can make pictures using your voice.

Stories have a narrator, an imaginary person, invented by the writer for the purpose of telling the story. First-person narrators participate in or are eyewitnesses to the story events. Third-person narrators may be omniscient (they know everything there is to be known about the world of the story) or limited (they see only part of the world, as an individual does). The story may say explicitly who the narrator is, or it may not. But this narrator, however much or little you know about him or her, is your road into the story, because when you read the story, you take on the character of the narrator. So you need to decide how you respond to the narrator.

Another element to look at is how the story appeals to you. Good stories appeal to both the mind and the heart—they work neither entirely by logic, nor entirely by feeling. And whether it's humorous, tragic, romantic, or adventurous, a good story can broaden your understanding of what it means to be human, teach you something about life, inspire you, enrich you. So think about whether the story moves you in some way.

If it does, then you want to explore deeper and discover the story's theme, which is the story's point or its message. A theme is usually a generalization about life or human behavior or values; it is true, but not a truism; rather, it reflects the author's insight into the way things are that she or he wants to share with readers. Theme is an important part of a story's meaning and is developed throughout the story. And it is important to note that a story can have multiple themes and meanings.

Besides patterns and symbols in the story (which often point to the theme), certain parts of a story often refer fairly directly to the theme: the title, the beginning, and the very end. An important character's first and final words or thoughts are also likely to carry powerful indications of theme. The theme of a story may never be explicitly stated, but it's what the story's about, what it means. These privileged places—along with the plot, the character, the setting, the mood, and the tone—all combine to create the thematic meaning of the story.

Choosing a story is different than choosing other material because many stories can be enjoyed on a surface level without a deep understanding of theme. The "meaning" of a story may come to someone later, after time and thought, or the person may simply continue to enjoy a well-constructed plot. Because of this, stories can be chosen to fit an audience with wide-ranging backgrounds—for example, families—without as much trouble as one might at first think.

Besides fairy tales, folk tales, myths, and tall tales, short stories by the following writers may provide you with material that you do not need to excerpt in order to use it for reading aloud.

Heinrich Böll	Ray Bradbury	Fray Angelico Chavez
Sandra Cisneros	Stephen Crane	O. Henry
Langston Hughes	Shirley Jackson	Ursula Le Guin
Jack London	Bernard Malamud	Guy de Maupassant
Saki	Isaac Bashevis Singer	Amy Tan
James Thurber	Anne Tyler	Kurt Vonnegut
Jessamyn West		

BRAIN TICKLERS
Set # 20

Find a story that you think would make good material for reading aloud and do the following for it:

1. Define the context.
2. Pre-read the text using the four steps on page 148.
3. Mark the text.
4. Read the text aloud pretending to be in front of an audience.

(Answers are on page 168.)

HELPFUL HINT

Sometimes reading aloud is a group activity—for example, reading a play in a literature class, doing an audition, reading a dialogue in a foreign language class, performing a reader's theatre piece, or doing a choral reading. Here are some pointers for reading with others.

1. **Follow along**. Follow along in the text while the other readers are reading. This way you won't lose your place.
2. **Pay attention to cues.** A cue is a signal to begin speaking. Your cue is the end of the line of the person speaking before you. The end of your line is the cue for the person speaking after you.
3. **Share the limelight.** Getting attention at the expense of the other performers is called **upstaging**. Learn to give and take individual focus as the main attention in the material shifts.
4. **Strive for balance.** "Freedom and Unity" is the Vermont State motto, and it's a great statement of the need to balance personal creativity and interpretation with what's going on in the rest of the group. The trick is to give the best you're capable of giving while working together to achieve a coherent whole.

Continued

There are a variety of ways to read with others. You may participate in the production of a play or musical with a director, cast, crew, and all the accoutrements. Or you may have a part in a smaller scale production such as a reader's theatre performance. Reader's theatre is defined in several different ways and is sometimes used synonymously with chamber theatre, but the main point is that it is *presentational*, not *representational*. The piece to be performed is spoken, but there is no staging to accompany the dialogue. The actors are still, and the characterization takes place in the voice, without movement, costume, or make-up. The actors face the audience, not each other. Presentations may include scripts or narratives adapted to the theatre using a narrator.

Scripts

The structure of a play is built around conflict. The action is initiated by an **inciting incident** that generally takes place before the play begins. As the play starts, **exposition** introduces the essential background information, as well as characters, situations, and conflicts. (Exposition may be found throughout the play as well as at the beginning.) At the **point of attack**, the chain of events initiated by the inciting incident disrupts the status quo, the **major conflict** of the drama is revealed, and the **rising action** begins. Tensions that occur after the major conflict has been established and that block the **protagonist** from resolving this conflict are called **complications.** At the **crisis** or **turning point**, usually the point at which the main character's action or choice determines the outcome, the outcome becomes irreversible. This moment may or may not coincide with the **climax** or **high point** of the action. The **falling action** follows, and the play concludes with the **resolution** or **denouement** when whatever is going to be wrapped up is concluded and the story is finished.

Though many older plays were written with five acts, there are also scripts for one-act plays, two-act plays, three-act plays, individual scenes, and (debuting in 1977 in Louisville, Kentucky, at the Humana Festival of New American Plays) the ten-minute play created by John Jory. Screenplays are written in three acts.

The conflict in a play is different than that in fiction because a play (with a few notable exceptions, like *Our Town*) has no narrator. Therefore, the conflict is shown by the words and actions of the characters—the agents of the conflict—rather than told by an observer or participant. Each speech moves the action deeper into conflict or toward resolution.

When reading a script, one person should take on the role of reading the stage directions, a crucial element of the text. Keep in mind that most scripts are created first and foremost for full performance. When a script is presented in a simple reading—in the course of classroom work, in reader's theatre, and the like— then there will, of necessity, be elements left undeveloped. You may wish to consult an expert from a theatre department at a local college or university for more information.

You can look for plays by the following playwrights:

Cherie Bennett	Paddy Chayefsky	Anton Chekhov
William Gibson	A. A. Milne	Reginald Rose
William Shakespeare	Neil Simon	James Still
Thornton Wilder	Susan Zeder	

To listen to radio plays:
"Shoestring Radio Theatre Radio Drama Links"

 http://www.shoestring.org/srt_links.html

To find radio play scripts:
"Teachers on Wheels: Radio Plays"

 http://www.nald.ca/province/nfld/tow/towplays/ playcont.htm

BRAIN TICKLERS
Set # 21

Choose a play or a scene that you think would make good material for reading aloud in some context and enough people to read it with and do the following for it:

1. Define the context.
2. Pre-read the text using the four steps on page 148.
3. Mark the text.
4. Read the script aloud with your fellow actors, pretending to be in front of an audience.

(Answers are on page 168.)

Poetry

Poems make meaning through the ordering of sound with careful attention to pattern. They appeal to the senses and make the most of every single word, syllable, and sound. In order to work with poetry—first to analyze it and select it and then to prepare it for reading aloud—you need to have some basic facility with meter so that you can decide whether a poem is scannable and, if necessary, scan it. You also need to understand the wide range of sound patterns that we call rhyme.

The specific speech genre of the poem will tell you something—maybe a great deal—about its meter and rhyme scheme. So you should try to identify the poem's structure. A source you might seek out to help you is *Painless Poetry*. Then you will need to identify the kind of verse you are working with, by noticing the stanzas (if any) and line construction. If you are working with metered poetry, you will identify the meter, and then look at the rhythm of each line, noticing metrical variations. You will chart the rhyme scheme for the end rhymes, if they're used, and notice other uses of rhyme, including internal rhyme, alliteration, and assonance, among others. Then, you can look for other uses of sound that the poet takes advantage of.

SOME POETIC SOUND DEVICES

Onomatopoeia	words that imitate the sounds they name, such as *buzz* and *whirr*
Euphony	the use of smooth, flowing, harmonious sounds, usually vowel sounds and the so-called liquid consonants *l* and *r*
Cacophony	the use of harsh sounds such as /k/ and /tch/ to create noise that is meant to be heard as unpleasant
Long sounds	consonant blends take longer to say; the poet can use them to slow down a line

BRAIN TICKLERS—THE ANSWERS

Set # 14, pages 106–107

Answers will vary. **Possible responses:**

1. Speech genre: graduation address; letter structure; academic style; content: changes in education in the twentieth century; audience: a graduating class in an education department at a college or university; purpose: to confirm for a new generation of teachers the importance of education in the United States.

2. Speech genre: personal letter; letter structure; colloquial style; content: a calico cat named Sheba; purpose: to inform and amuse a friend with a description of Sheba.

3. Speech genre: diary entry; letter structure; colloquial style; contents: events of the day; purpose: to relieve tension by committing the disconcerting events of the day to paper.

4. Speech genre: official government proclamation (specifically, this is the Emancipation Proclamation); proclamation structure; government style; content: freeing the slaves; purpose: to inform the country and world of the executive act by which the slaves have been freed and to persuade all who might think to defy the proclamation that they do so at the risk of military action from the government of the United States in support of the freedom of any former slave.

5. Speech genre: joke; dialogue structure; colloquial style; content: nonsense repetitions until the end when there is a surprising "sense"; purpose: to trick the other person into saying "I am a monkey."

Set # 15, page 112

Possible response:

HEAD LEVEL	HEADS	CHARACTERISTICS
CHAPTER TITLE	Chapter two "Confer, Converse, and Otherwise Hobnob": Informal Talk with Others	The word *chapter* and the number are in a fancy font, all caps, centered, and red. The title is in the same font, with important words having initial caps, centered, and red, and it is larger.
SUBHEAD	HOW DOES COMMUNICATION HAPPEN? THE ART OF CONVERSATION	In a thick sans-serif font, all caps, centered, and red, with a gray, dashed underscore, smaller than the chapter title.
SUB-SUBHEAD 1	A moment of understanding The idea of an "utterance" Speech genres Looking from the same perspective Orality vs. literacy Understanding the communication circle Maintaining a good attitude Talking about feelings Three kinds of conversation	In a plain sans-serif font, with only the first letter capped, flush left, and red, smaller than the subhead.
SUB-SUBHEAD 2	The role of the listener Communication over time Utterance defined Presuppositions It all depends on your point of view: Deixis Levels of engagement Face-to-face conversation	In a plain sans-serif font, with only the first letter capped, flush left, and black, smaller than the first sub-subhead.

HEAD LEVEL	HEADS	CHARACTERISTICS
	Phone conversation Instant messaging (or chat programs)	
SUB-SUBHEAD 3	Starting a conversation with someone you don't know After the introductions Etiquette in conversation Phone etiquette Phone messages But where's the voice? IM etiquette	In a serif font, with only the first letter capped, indented, and black, and slightly smaller than the sub-subhead 2.

Set # 16, pages 117–120

1. a. iii. **Possible response**: The ellipsis points show a semantic pause—I think she's really angry, and the exclamation point shows her emphasis through the polite word, *please*.

   b. iii. Since there are multiple aunts, there must not be a comma before *Susie*; since there is only one uncle, there may or may not be a comma before *Henry*. The material in quotation marks should be limited to the word *Huck*. The choice between dashes and parentheses is hard to make—one might argue for either. The exclamation point or lack of it could also be argued.

2. a. **Possible response**: Paine uses typography—both capitalization and italics—to indicate specific words to stress. His long sentences are well thought out and logically organized, and the structure is clearly indicated by his use of punctuation, which is a good guide to pauses. His parenthetical remarks delineated by commas ("in this crisis," "like hell,") I would signal by a change of pitch. I would read a

couple of places differently than he has indicated: I would read as if substituting a colon for the comma after "yet we have this consolation with us," and as if deleting the parentheses around "*not only to* TAX." The only place I see orthography mattering is for " 'Tis" instead of "It is," so I would be careful to read it as written.

b. Paying attention to Poe's orthography called my attention to certain spellings that are now considered British English (*cheque, labour*) and certain words of foreign origin: *Monsieur, Dupin, meerschaum, francs,* and *escritoire.* I also noticed the use of "eh" as a sound to indicate a tag question, and the "puff" sound Dupin makes as he smokes his pipe. The use of the initial with a long dash to conceal the name of the person who is too important to have his (fictional) identity revealed, is a clever touch. Poe does not use typography to inform me about how to read the excerpt, but he uses commas and dashes extravagantly in the first half. I would contrast D's drawling, pause-marked teasing of G——with the long sentences in the final paragraph, particularly the final, multi-predicate sentence that shows the prefect tumbling over himself to leave the house.

Set # 17, pages 125–127

Possible response:

Typography: Franklin uses italics and capitalization to call attention to words that require stress.

Orthography: Franklin uses an apostrophe to show the pronunciation of the past participles *bak'd, purchas'd, conquer'd,* and *nurtur'd* without the *-ed* being pronounced as a separate syllable. I gather from this that at one time the *-ed* was pronounced. The only other use I noted was *Tho'* spelled without the final *ugh*, which does nothing for the pronunciation anyway. I noticed that *expence* was not spelled with an *s* and *favour* was spelled with a *u*, both of which I put down to British spelling.

Punctuation: I would substitute a colon for the comma after "upon this" in the first sentence and after "no more Use" in the last sentence of III. I also find some extra commas that suggest what seem to me to be unnecessary pauses, for example after "consider" in the first sentence of I.

Figurative Language: Franklin, himself, calls attention to his simile, comparing an Empire to a cake. "Mother Country" is a personification, as is "Friends of Liberty."

Idioms: "rising of Mobs" and "uses his Wife ill"

Irony: The tone of the whole is ironic. Franklin is describing in detail the British attitude and actions toward their American colonies but couching it as advice on how to destroy an empire, which is—needless to say—not the British Empire's intention.

Other Patterns: consonance in "Ships and Seamen" and "Bullets and Bayonets"

Set # 18, pages 136–137

Answers will vary. **Possible responses:**

1. The turnips were not on the *table*, but in the *bathtub*.

2. The turnips were not *stacked* on the table, but *piled* in the bathtub.

3. The turnips were both *piled in the bathtub* and *stashed in the linen cupboard*.

4. The chickens were neither *white* nor *brown*.

5. The chickens were neither *white nor brown*, but a delicate shade of *lavender*.

6. "In the progress of *politics*, as in the common occurrences of *life*, we are not only apt to *forget* the ground we have traveled over, but frequently neglect to *gather up experience* as we go." *The Crisis* Number III, Thomas Paine

7. "Those who expect to *reap the blessings* of freedom, must, like men, *undergo the fatigues* of supporting it." *The Crisis* Number IV, Thomas Paine

8. "There is a dignity in the *warm passions of a whig*, which is never to be found in the *cold malice of a tory*." *The Crisis* Number VI, Thomas Paine

9. "It is not a little remarkable that in every case reported by ancient history in which government has been established with deliberation and consent, the task of framing it has not been committed to an *assembly of men*, but has been performed by some *individual citizen* of preeminent wisdom and approved integrity." *Federalist Paper No. 38*, Madison

10. I didn't say to meet at the *green house*: I said, "Meet me at the *greenhouse!*"

Set # 19, page 154

Answers will vary. See Appendix C, page 273.

Set # 20, page 156

Answers will vary. See Appendix C, page 277.

Set # 21, page 160

Answers will vary. See Appendix C, page 280.

CHAPTER FOUR

Composing a Speech

"It's a flat failure," said the speaker of his short speech. "The ceremony was rendered ludicrous" by the speaker's poor presentation, commented the correspondent from the London *Times*. "Anyone more dull and commonplace it would not be easy to produce." And yet, the hour and fifty-seven minute featured address on that occasion by Edward Everett, former governor of Massachusetts, is long forgotten. And the failure? Why, you know it yourself! It's the Gettysburg Address, and President Lincoln was reportedly still fiddling with his 269 words while he waited to speak.

Since a good rate for platform speaking is 125 words per minute, we can estimate that President Lincoln spoke for about two minutes. This is, in fact, confirmed by Edward Everett's comment on the president's remarks in a letter he sent to Lincoln later: "I should be glad if I could flatter myself that I came as near to the central idea of the occasion, in two hours, as you did in two minutes." And this brings us to the key point of this chapter—no matter for what occasion you are preparing to speak, no matter for how brief or how long a period of time, no matter for what audience or on which subject, no matter in what style or using which particular speech genre—the goal of your preparation is to give you the scaffolding so that you can deliver an utterance. This point is so important that we're going to review what it means. One way to say it is that you should judge your communication by whether it is finalized (that is, answerable), and whether it completes your desire to express yourself on the given subject in the given context at the given time for the particular audience for which it is made (see pages 53–54 for more information). This means you must always be thinking of the "communication circle" (page 61) as you prepare and think of your listeners, not as passive recipients of your words, but as the next speakers in an ongoing conversation.

HELPFUL HINT

The vocabulary used to describe different kinds of speeches can be very confusing. This is partly because the word *extemporaneous* can mean either a speech for which you get to prepare or exactly the opposite: a speech that you give on the spot, impromptu, with little or no preparation time. In some contexts, like debate clubs, there may even be finer distinctions: fully prepared speeches, speeches with a moderate amount of preparation (extemporaneous speeches), and speeches with only the briefest time between learning the topic and having to speak to it (impromptu speeches). We're going to talk about only two categories: prepared speeches and unrehearsed speeches. In this chapter, you will learn in detail the steps for the process of starting from the idea stage and developing a fully-prepared speech.

SPEECH GENRE SELECTION

You may be looking at this page in response to a very specific assignment—a humorous speech titled "My First Time Behind the Wheel," a presentation called "How to Dribble and Shoot a Basketball," or an oral report on "Airport Security After 9/11." If so, you probably already have a fairly clear idea of your speech genre (and within that of content, style, and structure), and of the audience, purpose, and context of your speech. If this is the case, you may proceed to Identifying Tasks and Choosing a Graphic Organizer on page 190.

Now, I'm supposing if you're still with me on this page that you have a more general assignment for which you need to make decisions yourself, or that you're on your own time (not taking a course) and thinking about preparing a talk of some sort. There are many different angles from which to start your brainstorming process, and we'll explore several. Because purpose is so closely tied to the other elements of an utterance (people don't usually say to themselves, "I want to cheer someone up. Whom should it be?"), it is probably a good idea to start your brainstorming

process elsewhere. So we'll look at starting with audience, subject, and speech genre.

Starting with your audience

If you have an identified audience—perhaps classmates at school or a workgroup at your jobsite—you can start by copying and filling in (or *filling out*, depending on what dialect of English you speak) the body of the audience identification chart that follows (leave speech genre, structure, content, purpose, style, and context blank for now).

Because speech genres each carry a range of audiences, as soon as you have identified an audience, you have some idea of appropriate speech genres and appropriate subjects. You will probably not prepare an epic poem or a formal rebuttal for three-year-olds, nor are you likely speak to them about the effects of Dutch elm disease on the profile of American town centers or the need to rethink the solid waste plan in your county. In most cases, ideas about your audience will guide your decisions in a more positive way. If you're speaking to your class for example, unless you're going to create a pretend scenario, you can immediately sort through the list of speech genres on pages 95–96 and select the ones that fit your audience.

If you will be speaking to people who are close to you, you may not even have to give the subject much thought—you may already have a good sense of the interests that you and your audience share, and what you can talk about that will get and hold their attention. Perhaps they'd even be willing to hear about a topic they're not (yet) especially interested in, just because *you* are speaking about it!

AUDIENCE IDENTIFICATION CHART

Name:_____ Date:_____

Speech genre:_____ Structure:_____

Content:_____

Purpose (desired response):_____

Style:_____ Context:_____

AUDIENCE IDENTIFICATION

Who is your audience? (Write a detailed description.)

1. Describe the age range of your audience.

2. Is your audience hostile or friendly?

3. What can you expect that your audience already knows about the content of your speech?

4. How many people make up the audience?

5. Is your audience known to you or not? If known, in what capacity?

6. What is your audience's cultural/ethnic background?

7. In some ways, your audience may be like you. In some ways, your audience may not resemble you at all. Use this chart to help you think about how your audience is similar to and different from you. Then explain your answers.

Characteristic	The same as you	Different from you
attitudes		
beliefs		
values		
interests		
prior knowledge		
experience		
political views		
socioeconomic status		

Which of the factors may be important, given the content and purpose of your speech? Circle the factors that will shape how you prepare to speak to your chosen audience. Then write some observations about each one.

Attitudes

Beliefs

Values

Interests

Prior knowledge

Experience

Political views

Socioeconomic status

Finding an authentic purpose for a particular audience is essential. Even if your speech is "just an exercise" for a class, creating an utterance depends on having a response in mind. The more clarity you can bring to this key element of the relationship between you and your audience, the better guidance you will provide yourself for evaluating how to create the framework for your speech. Do you want your brother to feel that letting you borrow his mountain bike was the finest decision he ever made? Do you want a two-year-old to commit to keep his shoes on while you take him to the park? Do you want every one of your classmates to sign a petition requesting that the school buy a set of timpani for the orchestra? In each of the utterances mentioned, you might inform, persuade, express yourself, and entertain in order to achieve your purpose.

Generous Brother

Inform	Guess what! I won the bike race!
Persuade	I beat my best time on my old bike by 14 seconds racing on yours— your bike is just tops, and I wouldn't have won without it.
Express	I am so glad that you were generous enough to let me borrow your bike. You're really a great brother!
Entertain	You should have seen the leader when I passed him! He had this look on his face like, "Where'd she come from?!"

Shoeless Two-Year-Old

Inform	Now we're going to go to the park.
Persuade	If you can keep your shoes on the whole time we're at the park, then you can go barefoot once we get back to your house.
Express	I would be really happy if you could keep your shoes on today at the park.
Entertain	"Hi, Ben. I'm Mr. Shoe. Please don't take me off! I might get lost. Then I would be sad. Boo hoo hoo!"

Percussion-Deprived Classmates

Inform	To play authentic orchestra music, we need to have the drums known as timpani in our school.
Persuade	The orchestra without timpani would be like our jazz band sans its drum set. We wouldn't even think of that as a possibility. Why would we do to our orchestra what we wouldn't do to our jazz band?
Express	This means a lot to me as a percussionist—when I have to stand empty-handed and watch the rest of the orchestra play an incomplete piece, I feel sad and deprived, not just on my own behalf, but on the whole school community's behalf.
Entertain	But you better believe, when we get these timpani, *I* get to be the first one to play them—and you better believe, there's nowhere you can go in this school that you will not know that the timpani have arrived!

Starting with the content

Let's say that you already have a subject in mind. Perhaps you want to speak about your pet skunk. Or maybe you are planning to give some kind of response to reading or viewing *Romeo and Juliet*. If you start with a subject—no matter what kind—it will help shape your thinking about your purpose, audience, and speech genre. In fact, your subject may have shaped one or more of these elements already.

What kind of purpose might you have for writing about your pet skunk? This topic is open to a wide variety of purposes. Maybe you want to persuade others that skunks make wonderful pets, or you may want to share a funny story about what your skunk did to lessen the irrational bias you've observed against skunks. Perhaps you want to inform people about aspects of skunk life they probably know nothing about, or use skunks as an example to teach people about words that they use everyday that come from American Indian languages (*skunk* comes from the Algonquian language, as does *raccoon*) to underscore the influence of Indian culture.

Like the subject of skunks, there are many subjects that you can speak about with a wide variety of purposes. Your choice of purpose will be shaped by the audience and speech genre. Narrowed subjects, or subject matter stated as questions, are often more closely tied to a particular purpose. *Athletic scholarships* is a fairly open subject. *How important are athletic scholarships?* requires evaluative thinking and suggests an audience who might receive athletic scholarships, donate to them, or be in some other way influenced by their existence, as well as a purpose of getting the audience to think or commit to some attitude about athletic scholarships.

Starting with speech genre

Here are the names of kinds of speeches using vocabulary employed in some speech classes and the speech genres that match. If you're not in a speech class, just look at the right-hand column to get some ideas—most people either have a couple of favorite speech genres, or can find one they'd like to try out.

MATCHING SPEECH CLASS VOCABULARY TO SPEECH GENRES

Speech class title	Speech genres that fit
speech to inform	biographical study demonstration directions history

Continued

Speech class title	Speech genres that fit
	how-to proposal research report
speech to persuade (convince; give an opinion)	argument case study commentary editorial political platform response or rebuttal review (book, movie, etc.)
speech to entertain	anecdote joke poem roast story
speech of personal experience	anecdote autobiography demonstration how-to monologue slide show
speech to stimulate or arouse an audience	address dedication eulogy invocation prayer promotion rally speech

Because, as we noted (see pages 100–105), speech genres carry an implicit range of appropriate content, audiences, and purposes, once you choose a speech genre—if this is how you start—you're well on your way.

SUBJECT DEVELOPMENT

Whatever way you make your initial approach, sooner or later you need to choose a subject to form the content of your speech. Here are three brainstorming methods to help you get going.

Thinking your way to a subject

You may find this chart useful in generating subject ideas.

FINDING SUBJECTS FROM FIELDS OF KNOWLEDGE

Field of knowledge	Categories
literature	• types of • authors • movements • of different cultures • over time • individual works
technology	• inventions • over time • inventors • Internet and society
science	• fields of • discoveries • scientists • health care • professions • history of • current problems
history	• of places • of peoples • of wars • of countries • political

Continued

Field of knowledge	Categories
government	• forms of • symbols of • history of • examples of • departments of • individual rulers • relationships between and among • wars • spying
athletics	• in schools • kinds of • sports teams • particular competitions • effects on life • history of • scholarships
social	• etiquette • communication • entertainment • music • theatre • television • movies • psychology

Shaking an idea loose

Another way to get an idea is to go through a random, haphazard list until something clicks for you. This can be done verbally or visually. Try verbally first.

airplanes	steel	inventions
rockets	graphic design	magic
pyramids	purple	castles
Matisse	cars	trains
plumbing	recreation	folklore
holidays	technology	apartheid
mountains	moon	dancing
Hamlet	dynamite	musicals
religion	gardens	libraries
Albania	crocodiles	crafts
cuisine	costumes	pets
sit coms	astrology	electric eels
pioneers	Hawaii	photography
dragons	zoos	architecture
pickling	tsars	choreography
Sacajawea	soccer	musical instruments
cartoons	rodents	Mississippi River
ethics	fireworks	seeing eye dogs
stars	dinosaurs	Loch Ness monster
pigs	gems	cancer
myths	alphabet	cartography
crafts	rabbits	democracy
tools	Olympics	Babylon
hats	fishing	brain
Egypt	computers	paleontology
business	perfume	silent movies
ocean	farms	orienteering
infancy	pests	transportation
robots	communication	garlic

Anything grab your attention? If not, try the visual form.

BRAIN TICKLERS
Set # 22

1. Either starting from an assignment, using one of the methods suggested, or by some formulation of your own, come up with a subject, audience, purpose, and speech genre for your speech.
2. Copy and fill in the audience identification chart on pages 174–175. Fill in as much of the top as you can at this time.

(Answers are on page 217.)

Narrowing your subject—The question approach

Because of the complexity of processing or decoding speech communication, 125 words per minute is *the* comfortable speed for platform speech. So you will have to narrow your subject sufficiently to make sure that you can actually state an utterance in the time allotted—because, if you can't say something finalized, something that is complete and answerable, the circle of communication is broken before it's even established. Other reasons to keep your content under control is to keep research manageable and to have a subject that both you and your audience will be able to recollect with ease—you so that you can deliver your speech and your audience so that they can recall what you said after they leave the performance space.

How much to narrow for your speaking time is not an exact science. There is no guide to tell you "for a five- to six-minute speech, choose this particular narrowness of subject." You will choose a subject and then work with it to discover what you can do with it in that time, given the way you speak. How you narrow it will depend a great deal on your audience, your purpose, your speech genre, and the context of your speech.

HELPFUL HINT

Here are four criteria to help you narrow your subject.

1. Do you have reason to believe that you have access to sufficient material to support your subject?
2. Is the subject appropriate to you, your audience, and the context? Consider whether your subject may be too technical, too banal, too unimportant, or too broad.
3. Do you believe your narrowed subject can be the focus of an utterance in the time allowed?
4. Do you know enough about the subject already that you will have sufficient time for preparation, given the performance date (if there is one)?

When we narrow a subject, we can look at it in one of two ways—as a *thing in itself* or as a *thing in a context*. In the first case, we analyze its attributes, the defining characteristics that make it what it is. In the second case, we analyze its relationships to something outside itself. The chart shows how this works. (Note that not every question in the chart will work for every subject, but sometimes a question can be made to work by playing with the words a little to adapt it.)

NARROWING A SUBJECT: THE DEFINITIVE GUIDE

Category	Questions
Attributes—The subject in itself	
operational analysis	How do you do it? What is the story of it? How does it work? How does/did it happen? How is/was it made? What does it require for its operation?
structural analysis	What are its parts? What variations occur in it? What is it made of? What systems form it? What examples are there of it?
sensory analysis	What is the experience of it like? How does it move? How does it look? How does it feel or what textures, weight does it have? How does it sound/what pitch, volume, etc., does it emit and under what circumstances? How does it taste? How does it smell?
Context	
theoretical analysis	How does it demonstrate the theory of ____? How does it manifest the outlook/perspective of ____?
classification analysis	What categories does it fit into? Under which systems can it be classified?

Continued

Category	Questions
situational analysis	Where is it? Under what circumstances does it exist/come into existence? Why does it happen when/where it does?
relational analysis	What kinds of interactions take place between it and ____? What relationships exist between it and ____?
meaning analysis	What does it mean (and to whom)? How can it be interpreted? Why was it made?
thematic analysis	What do you associate with it? What are its major meaning strands?
cause-and-effect analysis	What are its causes? What are its effects? What events led up to it? What events result from it (and other precipitating factors)?
historical analysis	What other events happened at the same time? What events preceded and followed it? What relationships does it have with past, concurrent, and future events?
utilization analysis	What is its purpose? What are its uses? What has it been used for? What could it be used for?
response analysis	What actions, feelings, and beliefs arise in response to it? How does it change the way people think, feel, and act?

Category	Questions
problem/solution analysis	Is it capable of solution? How can it be solved? How can it be mitigated/assuaged? What can be done to change it? What can be done to eliminate it? How can some of its effects be abated? How can it be applied in a new context?
comparative analysis	What is it like and how? How does it differ from other, similar things? How is it similar to and different from ____? How are its relationships like other relationships? What is an analogy/metaphor for some aspect of it?
logical analysis	Why is it valid? How can it be justified? What reasons and examples support it?
emotional analysis	How do people (I) feel about it? Why do people (I) feel as they (I) do about it? What could change people's ideas/feelings about it? What will people do/believe as a result of their feelings about it?
evaluative analysis	What is its value? How important is "it" in relation to ____? How well does "it" accomplish ____? How important is "it" to ____? How important is it that "it" continue? From what perspective(s) does "it" have (not have) value?

BRAIN TICKLERS
Set # 23

Use the question approach or some other approach that you find useful to narrow your subject.

(Answers are on page 217.)

Identifying tasks and choosing a graphic organizer

After you identify a question to help you narrow your subject, you can use the following chart to identify a task that will form the basis (though not the entire matter) of your work and a graphic organizer to help you structure your research and your speech. Remember that a speech genre is hardly ever composed entirely of a single task; a task is often better used to describe a single passage or paragraph. Use the graphic organizer *only as it serves your purposes*, and use multiple graphic organizers, if necessary.

ANALYSIS, RELATIONSHIPS, TASKS, AND GRAPHIC ORGANIZERS

Type of Analysis	Relationship	Task/Graphic Organizer
comparative	differences or opposition	compare/contrast (type 1)
comparative	similarities	compare/contrast (type 2)
operational	thing and its change over time	define (type 1)
operational	thing and its function(s)	define (type 2)
structural	thing and its components/ examples of it	define (type 3)
sensory	thing and its attributes or description	define (type 4)
relational	thing and its (necessary) associations	define (type 5)
theoretical meaning thematic	thing and its meaning	define (type 6)
utilization	thing and its purpose(s)	define (type 7)
evaluative	thing and its value/thing measured by criteria	define (type 8)
situational	thing and its environment	define (type 9)

Continued

Type of Analysis	Relationship	Task/Graphic Organizer
any	conglomeration	list
logical	hypothesis	argue (type 1)
problem/ solution	problem & solution/ resolution/ amelioration	argue (type 2)
logical	proposition/ support or statement/proof	argue (type 3)
logical	question and answer	argue (type 4)
cause-and-effect response emotional	cause/effect	sequence (type 1)
historical	series of events in time	sequence (type 2)
classification	subordination	classify (type 1)

BRAIN TICKLERS
Set # 24

Using the preceding chart and the graphic organizers in Appendix A (pages 255–263),
identify one or more graphic organizers that
may be of use to you in researching and struc-
turing your paper.

(Answers are on page 217.)

RESEARCH AND SOURCES

What "researching" will mean for your speech will depend entirely on your choices. If you are planning to speak about a personal experience, research may mean no more than recalling the events in detail (or perhaps consulting a journal or a close friend). Research could also mean hours at the library and/or on the Internet. Decide what you need to do, based on your subject, and consult materials from these lists, if applicable.

USEFUL SOURCES ON THE INTERNET

Source type	Internet location
all kinds	http://www.refdesk.com/instant.html
newspapers	http://www.refdesk.com/papmain.html
encyclopedia	http://www.refdesk.com/myency.html
other reference	http://www.onelook.com/browse.shtml
quotations from literature	http://www.bartleby.com/

PRINT SOURCES

Source type	Title
almanacs	World Almanac and Book of Facts
dictionaries	Oxford English Dictionary
encyclopedias	Encyclopedia Britannica QPB Science Encyclopedia
handbooks	Ploetz's Manual of Universal History Political Handbook of the World
indexes	Poole's Index to Periodical Literature (up to 1906) Reader's Guide to Periodical Literature (since 1900)

Continued

Source type	Title
newspapers	*The Wall Street Journal* *The Washington Post* *The New York Times*
quotations	*Bartlett's Familiar Quotations* *Quotationary* *African American Quotations* *The Wisdom of the Native Americans* *The New Beacon Book of Quotations by Women* *Respectfully Quoted: A Dictionary of Quotations*
specialized dictionaries	*Funk & Wagnalls Standard Dictionary of Folklore, Mythology, and Legend* *Dictionary of American Slang* *A Dictionary of American Proverbs* *Dictionary of National Biography* *Dictionary of American Biography* *Who's Who in America* *Who's Who* *Webster's Biographical Dictionary* *Webster's New Geographical Dictionary*
yearbooks	*Britannica Book of the Year* *The American Yearbook*

For other sources, and for help doing on-line searches, ask your reference librarian. Some older periodicals will be available on microform or microfiche—again, the reference librarian can assist you.

Choosing good sources is important. You have to know what "good" means in the given context. Is the most current source the best? Often it is, but it may not be if you're researching, say, slang used in the 1960s. Do you want the most authoritative source? Always, but you may also want less authoritative sources for a variety of reasons—perhaps the authority refers to them, so you need to know what they say, or perhaps you will need to rebut their objections. It is not always easy to evaluate writers/thinkers in a field with which you're not familiar. Their credentials, a sense that they have mastery of the material, and a sense of integrity and intellectual honesty are signs to look for.

HELPFUL HINTS

Here are some tips for researching on the Internet:

1. Use a META SEARCH ENGINE—a search engine that searches on a group of other search engines—and ranks responses. The Advanced Search on Profusion is my favorite:

 http://www.profusion.com/default.asp?
agt=0!&cat=1!&cobid=ess&sid=
{F02A7CBF-39FE-4543-A00E-
A841B0C45D57}&queryterm=

2. If possible, use the search engine description to sort the wheat from the chaff and only go to the sites that look promising; skim material for relevance; and print the material so you can read it off-line. Spend your on-line time uncovering sources. This is especially important if you have limited computer time.

3. If the information you need on a page won't print (for example, white text on a black background doesn't print on some systems), sometimes you can copy and paste it into a document and print it from there. If you copy material from an Internet source to a document before printing it, ALWAYS COPY AND PASTE THE URL WITH IT so that you have the source.

Now that you've got your sources, what next? Read! Highlight or take notes (or both) as you read, and just become familiar with the subject so that you can take the next step: Take a shot at answering your question. Remember your question? If you've chosen your sources well, you've now got enough background and factual support to start building an answer, and this answer is the **thesis** of your speech. So, depending on which question you were focusing on, your thesis might turn out something like this:

- Architecture plays a symbolic role in the *Fellowship of the Rings* movie.
- The meaning of "Let's roll" became fixed forever as a patriotic cry of the free citizen defending his country on September 11, 2001.
- Analysis of the shopping scene in B____ reveals how organic and vegetarian food availability has influenced the buying habits of self-identified meat-and-potatoes consumers.

After you have identified your thesis, it is time to begin taking notes on the material you need to support your thesis.

When taking notes on research materials, many people find it easiest to note each bit of information on a separate index card, on which is indicated the source of the information. (You need the source information both in case you want to return to the original source for some reason and in order to credit the information, if necessary, in your speech, so record the details, including page numbers, carefully.) This system allows you to shuffle the cards into various orders to try different organizations for your speech. A heading on each note card will help when it's time to group them.

Architecture and lighting—general comment

Lord of the Rings: The Fellowship of the Ring reviewed by Charity Bishop
http://www.charitysplace.com/review/review-fellowship.htm

"The architecture and construction of the many sets, ranging from the dark and foreboding Orthanc (where the evil wizard dwells) to the brightly-lit Elfin city of Rivendell are nothing less than magical. Lighting creates a mood; the places inhabited by good are often bright and cheering, or subtly blue in the darkness; places dominated by evil are dark and foreboding, grotesque, chilling."

COMPOSING YOUR SPEECH

The president is about to deliver a speech, and you know he's got every single carefully chosen word in front of him on the teleprompter. So maybe you think that's what preparing a speech is—getting everything in order so that you can *read* your speech. Well, that is, in fact, what some people do. And, let's face it, when national security and world peace are on the agenda, saying things "just so" is absolutely crucial.

But some people feel gypped by speakers who read their words. They want the sense of presence and involvement that comes from two people who meet in conversation and are not only meeting face-to-face but also making eye contact. That's why the president uses a teleprompter instead of a written copy of the speech and works really hard to look natural and conversational when, actually, every word, every intonation, is carefully crafted. You might think that memorizing your speech is a possible answer. But there are problems with that approach, too. When you actually meet your audience, if you've misjudged them or the context at all, your early slant will make it evident that you're here-and-now talk is actually prefabricated. And—what if you lose your place, forget your lines, blank on what comes next? There's a better way, say the speech experts.

First of all, it's probably a pretty good shot that whatever subject you're trying to master and share, it's at least a *little* less crucial than the fate of the nation as told by the commander in chief.

Second, there's a middle way between memorizing your speech and reading it word for word. Speaking from notes—either an outline, your graphic organizer, or a large note card (or several small ones if you prefer)—can give you the best of both worlds, plus an added advantage that neither of the other methods has.

WHY SPEAK FROM NOTES WITHOUT MEMORIZING?

Advantage like reading	Advantage like memorizing	Additional advantage
You have at your fingertips any material that you must have verbatim for accuracy (e.g., quotations).	You can make a lot of eye contact with your audience, not be always looking at material.	You speak from your knowledge of your material (not just your knowledge of a particular set of words about that material), adapting your speech to the events, insights, and reactions you receive *as you speak*.

BRAIN TICKLERS
Set # 25

1. If your subject requires it, do appropriate research to find material for your speech. Read through your material and identify a thesis statement that answers your question. Write your thesis statement.
2. Take notes to support the speech you will give on your thesis.

(Answers are on page 217.)

Supporting your thesis

To prove or support your thesis, you must back it up with some of the information you garnered from your research. Ten kinds of support for your thesis include:

1. Statistics
2. Specific facts
3. Interview material
4. Studies
5. Surveys
6. Quotation of authority opinion
7. Examples
8. Anecdotal evidence
9. Audience activity such as a survey, demonstration, or quiz
10. Trends

You will arrange your support in some logical order, one of the basic organizing patterns that are used in speechcraft.

ORGANIZING PATTERNS (THIS LIST IS NOT EXHAUSTIVE)

Compare/contrast	categorical
Define	spatial
List	specific to general general to specific
Argue	importance (increasing or decreasing)
Sequence	step-by-step chronological
Classify	categorical

BRAIN TICKLERS
Set # 26

Choose an organizing pattern and arrange your notes in the order you have decided upon.

(Answers are on page 217.)

Filling in your graphic organizer(s) and outlining

Filling in your graphic organizer(s) and outlining are two means to the same end: finding and organizing the key points that support your thesis in a form from which you can speak. Opinion is divided on whether you should use complete sentences (sentence outline) or phrases (topic outline), so experiment to see what works best for you. Here are the rules for how to construct an outline:

1. Use the headings on your note cards to group related ideas together.
2. Identify the main points that support your thesis. Each main point becomes a main topic in your outline and is identified by a Roman numeral followed by a period.
3. Subtopics of diminishing importance are indented and identified with (in this order) capital letters, Arabic numerals, small letters, Arabic numerals in parentheses, and small letters in parentheses. There must be a minimum of two subtopics to support the preceding topic. With the exception of numerals and small letters in parentheses, each subtopic identifier is followed by a period.
4. Capitalize the first word of each topic. In a sentence outline, end with a period. In a topic outline, do not use end punctuation.

5. Usually, topics of the same importance are parallel in construction.
6. Usually, no less than three main points are necessary to support a thesis.

NOTE

Some speech teachers have students create separate outlines for the introduction, body, and conclusion of their speech so that they can clearly see these important structural divisions. Feel free to do this unless you are preparing for a class and have been instructed otherwise. In this case, you may not need to have more than one main point in your introduction or conclusion.

Models of Outline Form

TITLE

I.
  A.
    1.
    2.
  B.
    1.
    2.
    3.
II.
  A.
    1.
    2.
      a.
      b.
        (1)
        (2)
          (a)
          (b)
  B.
III.
  A.
  B.
IV.
  A.
    1.
    2.
    3.
  B.
V.
  A.
  B.
  C.

TITLE

INTRODUCTION
I.
  A.
    1.
    2.
BODY
I.
  A.
    1.
    2.
      a.
      b.
        (1)
        (2)
          (a)
          (b)
  B.
    1.
    2.
II.
  A.
  B.
  C.
III.
  A.
  B.
CONCLUSION
I.
  A.
  B.

Here is an outline of part of this chapter for demonstration purposes. You may compare it to the actual text.

COMPOSING A SPEECH

I. Speech genre selection
   A. Starting with your audience
   B. Starting with the content
   C. Starting with speech genre
II. Subject development
   A. Thinking your way to a subject
   B. Shaking an idea loose
   C. Narrowing your subject—the question approach
   D. Identifying tasks and choosing a graphic organizer
III. Research and sources
IV. Composing a speech

Notice that the outline points have, in this case, translated into the headings in the text. Also note that this is *not* the outline that I started with. As I developed the chapter, the outline changed. This will also happen to you, so be prepared, and consider making your outline in pencil. You can see the parallel construction by looking at the first word of each of the subtopics. You can also see that I chose to use a topic outline, rather than a sentence outline.

BRAIN TICKLERS
Set # 27

Construct an outline for your speech. For right now, you can leave out the introduction and conclusion—they require special attention, and we'll focus on them in a bit. Just get the body of your speech organized.

(Answers are on page 217.)

Looking for tasks

HELPFUL HINT

At some point, you need to decide whether you will speak from your outline or graphic organizer. Since many people speak from outlines, I'm going to use that as a reference, but if you prefer to use the graphic organizer, just substitute that in your mind.

The next step is to check your outline to identify any portions that can be fairly clearly identified as fitting into the six task categories: compare/contrast, define, list, argue, sequence, classify. After you identify the task, refer to the chart on pages 131–134 to identify words that can have a key function in helping the listener construct a meaningful understanding of what you're saying. Using a colored pencil or marker, write these key words and phrases in appropriate places between points on your outline to show the logical relationships.

The composition process

Now that you're done with the body part of your outline, you can start composing your speech. Notice, I didn't say start *writing* your speech. There's a good reason for that. If you sit down and write your speech, unless you're an extraordinarily gifted writer, you're going to end up with a major clash of orality and literacy. All the conventions you've been taught for writing are just for that—for writing. But now, you're trying to put together something to speak, not something that has to meet the standards for written prose. Remember the things we said about the differences between orality and literacy (pages 59–60) and about the conventions in prose (like emoticons) that substitute (poorly) for the elements of paralanguage that aren't captured on paper (pages 78–81)?

- Written sentences can be more complex than spoken sentences, and readers have more time to think and review than listeners.
- Written sentences are not planned to be interactive, so writers try to anticipate readers' responses and incorporate them.
- Readers can process more information than listeners.
- Listeners have less recall than readers.

So here's what you can do: you can make up your speech out loud and *then* write it down. Oh, you might refine the language in your writing, make it a little more literary. But by *starting* with oral language, you can make sure that you're attuned to the needs of your audience.

BRAIN TICKLERS
Set # 28

With your outline in hand, stand up, and start talking. Having a timer handy will help you make a judgment about how long the material will be once you add your introduction and conclusion. Do this three times. Make notes after each trial. It's okay if you say different words each time. It's also okay if some words start to gel and remain the same each time.

(Answers are on page 217.)

REFINING YOUR SPEECH

Now that you've said words out loud, you can really say you've got the beginnings of a speech. Next, you need to check your logic and language, add an introduction and conclusion, and come up with one or more visual aides, if appropriate.

Logic and logical fallacies

A **logical fallacy** is a faulty argument in which something besides reason contributes to the conclusion drawn. Many fallacies have been named and categorized to make them easier to recognize and remember.

Two basic forms of reasoning are deduction and induction.

Deductive reasoning moves from the general to a specific instance of the general cases being considered. If something is true in general, and an instance is really representative of that general class, then the truth will hold for the specific instance. Syllogisms are examples of deductive reasoning.

STANDARD SYLLOGISM FORM

> Every X is Y. (All flowers are plants.)
> C is X. (A columbine is a flower.)
> Therefore, C is Y. (Therefore, a columbine is a plant.)

Fallacies in deductive reasoning come about when one of the first two statements of a syllogism is not true, for example, if C is assumed to be a member of X when it truly isn't.

Inductive reasoning moves from the particular to the general. It is harder to achieve certainty with this kind of logic because you have to determine when you've looked at enough particular examples to be able to draw a general rule that will hold good in all cases.

This is not a complete list of logical fallacies, but it includes some of the more common ones.

SOME LOGICAL FALLACIES

Insufficient evidence

hasty generalization—drawing a conclusion with too little evidence

fallacy of exclusion—leaving out evidence that would change the outcome of an inductive argument

oversimplification—making a complex issue simple by ignoring some of its aspects

Cause-and-effect mistakes

Gambler's due—assuming that after a certain number of events of a similar kind, things are "due" to change

post hoc, ergo propter hoc—literally "after this, therefore, on account of it"; assuming that something that comes after is caused by what came before

slippery slope—assuming that one thing inevitably leads to another

false analogy—assuming that because of some (superficial) resemblances, conclusions drawn from one case apply to another

Emotion rather than reason

appeal to hate—claiming that if people don't like an idea, it should be dismissed

appeal to force—attempting to persuade the listener/reader by threat or actual force

guilt by association—inferring that a person's character can be discovered by looking at the company s/he chooses

special pleading—presenting a case as being outside the rules (can contain a more specific appeal to emotion, such as **appeal to pity**)

BRAIN TICKLERS
Set # 29

Check your current set of notes and review the body of your speech. Is your logic valid? If not, rethink your arguments, returning if necessary to your research to find additional (or better) support for your points, or even changing your points. Redo anything that needs redoing.

(Answers are on page 217.)

Vivid language and voice

Using figurative language (pages 122–123) is a means of heightening your language. If you use figurative language, make sure that you employ devices that your audience will be able to interpret at listening speed without the benefit of "looking back."

Sensory language engages the senses of sight, hearing, smell, taste, and touch by using images that appeal to the senses. Sight is the sense most often invoked, and taste is usually exercised the least. Sensory language helps people imagine the scene in the "movie" in their minds.

On the other hand, words like *smart, good, nice, said, sure, see, fix, wonderful, awful, terrible, get, old, mad, interesting, funny, pretty, like,* and *very* are overused, and substituting a synonym is usually an excellent idea. Try a thesaurus for ideas.

Quotations don't just support your thesis, they can add piquant, evocative language to your speech, and because they're someone else's words and phrasing, they change the pace and style for a moment or two. If you find an apt quotation, use it. For examples, see the speeches of Robert F. Kennedy and Ronald Reagan in Appendix B (pages 268 and 270).

Caution—Major Mistake Territory!

Make sure that any changes you make, reflect *your* voice and *your* range of oral language use. The authenticity and "you-ness" of the language in your speech is essential for you to succeed in conveying your utterance. This does not mean that you shouldn't try anything new. It does mean that you shouldn't load your speech with other people's ideas of exciting language that will thrill an audience because then it will no longer be *your* speech.

Your introduction

At some moment, by some indication—dimming lights, an announcement, your appearance—a hush falls over the room. It is the moment that everyone has been waiting for. What happens now is up to you. What are you going to do with this moment?

The purpose of your introduction is to gain attention *for your specific utterance*. Therefore, your introduction must make a connection between you and your audience in some way that is pertinent to the particular context. There are many ways to arouse interest: this one must be focused to lead your audience into your speech.

Here are some tried and true approaches to arousing an audience's interest. Each is useful in particular circumstances.

- State clearly the context, occasion, and purpose of the gathering.
- Open with a story or anecdote or joke linked to the subject of the speech.
- Explain why you chose to speak on the particular subject you did, complimenting the audience on some quality that ties into the speech subject, if appropriate.
- Provide background information (about yourself or your subject) that is necessary to an understanding of what is to come.
- Refer to an incident with which the audience is familiar (for example, a local event or something that happened earlier in the day).
- Begin with a quotation that shows great insight, cites a recognized authority, or that you wish to refute.
- Set out a striking idea.
- State an arresting fact.
- Ask the audience a question.
- Give the audience something to ponder, which, as you tell them, you will return to at the end of your speech.
- Begin your story *in medias res* (in the middle of things) as the poet Horace recommended or in some exciting or tantalizing way.

Whatever method you use, make sure that the tone of your introduction is consistent with the tone of the body of your speech. You should not, for example, be sincere in one and sarcastic in the other.

BRAIN TICKLERS
Set # 30

Compose an introduction for your speech. In other words, come up with an idea, and speak it, continuing into the body of your speech until you are satisfied that it fits.

(Answers are on page 217.)

Your conclusion

Before you compose your conclusion, reread the section about the finalization of an utterance on pages 53–54. This section of your speech is extremely important because it is the transition between your utterance and your audience's response. Some speech experts suggest that your conclusion should be no more than one-eighth to one-tenth of the total length of your speech. Nevertheless, it is the last of your words that the audience will hear; and, therefore, the words they are most likely to remember. So ask yourself, "What do I most want people to remember?"

BRAIN TICKLERS
Set # 31

Look at the conclusion of every speech in Appendix B. Which, in your opinion, is the most memorable? Why?

(Answers are on page 217.)

Most written expository compositions end with a summary. This does not have to be so with a speech. You might summarize. But you also might

- reiterate the thesis of your speech in a new way, using a quotation from literature or poetry;
- add a final supporting insight or fact that you've saved;
- use an analogy to drive home your point;
- end with an anecdote that illustrates your meaning;
- call your audience to take action;
- request your audience to reconsider the point you asked them to ponder at the beginning of your speech;
- ask your audience if their answer to your initial question has changed; or
- invite your audience to ask questions or offer comments.

Your title

Your title should have the virtue of being either brief, clever, or both. It should, as succinctly as possible, let the audience know something about your thesis.

Remember these thesis statements (from page 196)? Here they are matched with possible titles:

Thesis statement	Possible title
Architecture plays a symbolic role in the *Fellowship of the Rings* movie.	You Are What You Build
The meaning of "Let's roll" became fixed forever as a patriotic cry of the free citizen defending his country on September 11, 2001.	Let's Roll
Analysis of the shopping scene in B___ reveals how organic and vegetarian food availability has influenced the buying habits of self-identified meat-and-potatoes consumers.	Tempeh Goes Mainstream

BRAIN TICKLERS
Set # 32

Brainstorm three titles for your speech. Choose your favorite.

(Answers are on page 217.)

Visual aides

You are, of course, the chief visual aide in your speech. Your face, hands, and body will express a great deal of your meaning. You may use gesture and even pantomime to get your points across. But there are other ways, too, to take advantage of the visual, as well as the aural, nature of a live presentation. Here are some ideas.

VISUAL AIDES

audio tape	chart
drawing	flip chart
graph	handout
list	overhead transparencies
photograph	prop
sample	slides
video clip	

HELPFUL HINTS

1. The visual aide is an aide; it's not the main event. Make sure to keep it in its place. Bring it out when it's called for, and put it out of sight when it's done so that it doesn't distract your audience's attention.

2. Make the visual aide as simple as possible. Unless it's in a handout that they will walk away with, the audience will only have a limited amount of time in which to view it.

3. If you make a graph, match the data to the graph type. Know the uses of pie charts, bar graphs, line graphs, and the like, and use them appropriately. Make sure that the visual aide is large enough and in a position so that everyone in the audience can easily see it.

4. Make sure that slides, overhead transparencies, and any other sets of sequenced items are in the correct sequence and facing in the proper direction.

5. Make sure that all electronic equipment is functioning.

6. Make sure that all audio- and/or videotapes are properly cued.

7. Make a plan B. The electricity could go out. The slide projector could blow a bulb. The tech department could fail to deliver the VCR.

8. Keep words on visual aides to a minimum—focus on the visual.

9. If your audience is looking at a handout, they're not looking at you. Only use a handout if absolutely necessary.

10. Don't put anything on a visual aide that you will not explicitly mention in your speech.

Before you create your visual aide, decide whether you want it to show something static (a relationship or system, for example) or whether you want it to show something dynamic (for example, a process), and plan accordingly. Choose whether you will bring in a visual aide that is already made, or whether you will create the aide in front of the audience (on a flip chart or transparency, for example, or perhaps in response to audience input). Always practice your speech out loud, using (or making) the aide so that you are comfortable handling it.

BRAIN TICKLERS
Set # 33

Think of a visual aide that will enhance your speech. Find it, create it, or plan it, depending on its nature.

(Answers are on page 217.)

How do you know when you're done? (finalization)

As you work through the composing process, as well as preparation and delivery, keep asking yourself if your choices are working toward achieving an utterance. Do you think that when you deliver this speech, you will have said all you wanted to say to this audience at this time, in this context, and that they will be able to respond to you?

BRAIN TICKLERS—THE ANSWERS

Set # 22 through Set # 30

Answers will vary.

Set # 31, page 212

Answers will vary. **Possible response:** I was stirred deeply by the quotation President Reagan used to end his speech.

Set # 32 and Set # 33

Answers will vary.

CHAPTER FIVE

Practicing and Performing
"Think All You Speak"

"Think all you speak, but speak not all you think. Your thoughts are your own; your words are so no more."

—Dean Patrick Delany

Irish Clergyman (1685?–1768), Dean of Down

This chapter gives you both all-purpose advice about public speaking and detailed and specific hints for the kinds of specialized situations that will come out of plans you have made for a performance in reading aloud (in Chapter 3) or speaking (in Chapter 4). It concludes with some suggestions for evaluation that will help you to use each occasion to improve your next presentation.

PRACTICING PREPARED MATERIAL

Speaking to others is so natural. And performance is natural, too—look at young children and how they carry on when company comes to visit. Understanding and learning techniques that enhance communication in presentation situations does not make our communication artificial, any more than taking lessons to learn how to play an instrument depreciates our "natural abilities." Learning to use the instruments we have for communication—our body and voice—allows us to communicate more deliberately, and thus gives us more control over our utterances. To be effective, our practice must be as authentic as possible, so practice for performance should be done out loud. There is no denying the value in silently visualizing your performance prior to speaking as well as athletic and other events. Nevertheless, oral performance requires oral practice.

Stance

Our voices depend on air, and the posture of our bodies determines how efficiently our airflow moves. It is best to practice in whatever position you will take when you perform. Since most public speaking is done from a standing position, here is a description of a starting posture, from which you will, of course, move or deviate when appropriate or necessary.

Stand with your feet under your hips and your weight balanced on both feet. If you wish, you may place one foot slightly in front of the other and put slightly more weight on the forward foot. You need not be stiff, but you should hold yourself at your full height. Your hands may hang loosely at your sides or you may hold your notes quietly in one hand between your thumb

and forefinger. When you need to see your notes, lift them into your line of sight so that you do not have to bend your head. If possible, avoid using a podium or stand because it puts a large obstacle between you and your audience. If you must speak from behind a stand, place your notes carefully and make sure that they are well lit.

Breathing

In order for you to speak, you need air. Try this: Inhale and speak at the same time. Can't make very much sound, can you? That's because you need the outward movement of air to vibrate the vocal cords in order to make speech sounds (see page 9). Now exhale as much as you can, out of both your nose and your mouth and then try to speak. You probably can't produce a sound with much quality. You not only need air, you need it in quantity to make quality sound. So take good full breaths.

For your breath to work for you, it has to come from deep inside you. Some people make the mistake of breathing from the throat instead of the diaphragm. Try this exercise.

BREATHE DEEPLY
Place your notes on the seat of a chair that is moderately heavy. Lift the chair, hold it at arm's length, breathe, and begin your speech. Pay attention to what your breathing feels like. Put down the chair and try to breathe in the same way as you continue speaking.

Also try to make your breathing as inaudible as possible. Especially if you're going to be using a microphone, you don't want people focusing on your breathing noises. Hisses and squeaks can be caused by breathing in through both the nose and mouth and by the position of the mouth when breathing. If you shape your mouth as if you were going to say *eat* and breathe in, you'll probably hear some noise. Try it. Now, shape your mouth to say *oh* and try breathing in again. What do you hear? You should hear less noise, maybe silence.

If you are reading aloud, you may find it helpful to read ahead a few words. This and practicing will help you plan places to breathe that fit naturally with the text—natural pauses for meaning, often those marked by punctuation marks are best. If you need to, review the section on punctuation in Chapter Three (pages 113–117 and 137–138). You may find it helpful to mark breathing spots.

BRAIN TICKLERS
Set # 34

Try out the breathing exercises. Can you breathe silently?

(Answers are on page 251.)

General speaking drills

If our utterances are have any effect, our individual words must be understood. Good **enunciation**, or **articulation**, shapes our breath with care so that others can interpret out speech easily. Here are some speech drills to help you develop clear and accurate enunciation. For the best results, do the starred exercises with someone who doesn't know what you're reading and see if s/he can understand you.

HARD TO READ
Slowly read a piece of writing, hitting the hard consonant sounds (*b, ch, d, g, k, p,* and *t*) and overenunciating each syllable. Start slowly, and build up speed.

PENCIL DRILL*

Read a piece of writing with a pencil placed horizontally between your teeth.

BUBBLE GUM FUN*

Chew about five sticks of chewing gum, and then try reading aloud. You'll discover just how clearly you can speak. No fair sticking the gum in your cheek!

SDRAWKCAB LLIRD

Try reading backwards, word by word. Then read the same material forwards.

READING A IS A FUN A

Say the word *a* after each word to help prevent slurring.

TONGUE TWISTERS

Now here's a fun way to increase your verbal agility. The one-liners come first, followed by the poems.

Black background, brown background.
Eddie edited it.
Flash message!
Green glass globes glow greenly.
Lovely lemon liniment.
Roberta ran rings around the Roman ruins.
Rubber baby buggy bumpers.
Six sleek swans swam swiftly southwards.
Stupid superstition!
The great Greek grape growers grow great Greek grapes.
The sixth sick sheik's sixth sheep's sick.
Three short sword sheaths.
Toy boat. Toy boat. Toy boat.
World Wide Web

Betty Botter

Betty Botter had some butter,
"But," she said, "this butter's bitter.
If I bake this bitter butter,
it would make my batter bitter.
But a bit of better butter—
that would make my batter better."

So she bought a bit of butter,
better than her bitter butter,
and she baked it in her batter,
and the batter was not bitter.
So 'twas better Betty Botter
bought a bit of better butter.

The Thistle-Sifter

Theophiles Thistle, the successful thistle-sifter,
in sifting a sieve full of un-sifted thistles,
thrust three thousand thistles through the thick of his thumb.

Now. . . if Theophiles Thistle, the successful thistle-sifter,
in sifting a sieve full of un-sifted thistles,
thrust three thousand thistles through the thick of his thumb,
see that thou, in sifting a sieve full of un-sifted thistles,
thrust not three thousand thistles through the thick of thy thumb.
Success to the successful thistle-sifter!

The Toads

A tree toad loved a she-toad
Who lived up in a tree.
He was a two-toed tree toad
But a three-toed toad was she.
The two-toed tree toad tried to win
The three-toed she-toad's heart,
For the two-toed tree toad loved the ground
That the three-toed tree toad trod.
But the two-toed tree toad tried in vain.
He couldn't please her whim.
From her tree toad bower
With her three-toed power
The she-toad vetoed him.

The Night-Light

You've no need to light a night-light
On a light night like tonight,
For a night-light's light's a slight light,
And tonight's a night that's light.
When a night's light, like tonight's light,
It is really not quite right
To light night-lights with their slight lights
On a light night like tonight.

BRAIN TICKLERS
Set # 35

Try out the enunciation exercises. Which work best for you?

(Answers are on page 251.)

Mirror or recording

It is often advised to practice while looking in the mirror. This may or may not work for you. Looking into one's own eyes can be disconcerting. The idea is to bring to your attention habitual postures, gestures, and other body language that may distract your audience or that you may for other reasons wish to eliminate before your performance. After all, you want your audience's attention to be focused on what you want to say to them, not be inadvertently drawn to some other locus. With this in mind, you may want to put on the outfit you plan to wear when you do your mirror or recording practice. Then you can see yourself as your audience will see you.

If you have the opportunity to be videotaped, by all means, take advantage of it. Even if you are nervous, you will obtain a much better indication of your performance behavior than you will looking into your own gaze in the mirror.

Practicing with an audience

If what you're trying to do is communicate with other people, why practice talking to yourself? It really doesn't make much sense does it? How can you make judgments about the quality of your communication unless and until you try it out on an audience? Even though it won't be the same audience under the same circumstances, it will still begin to let you know if you've achieved an utterance. If the folks listening to you *now* can respond to you as you wish, you need to know that. If they can't, why, you need to know that, too! If you have the opportunity, practice at least once in the performance space. This will allow you to become familiar with the "feel" of the space and also the particular sound. If the space was created for performance, your voice may sound very different than it does in a room in a house or in a classroom. Spaces also have different sounds when they are empty and when they are filled with people. Make your practices as similar to the real event as possible.

Transitions

One of the important things to practice with an audience is your transitions. Whether you are reading a story or delivering a speech, you need to keep your audience aware of where in the structure they are. In a well-written story that follows standard form, the audience will have a fairly easy time determining beginning, middle, or end. In a speech, you need to be careful to bring your audience through your structure with you.

- Remember to stress the transition words you built into your notes. These words will help your audience recognize portions of your speech in which you accomplish the six familiar tasks.
- A visual aid can summarize or forecast, if appropriate.
- A pause and a breath can help make a transition between major points, as can a change of position in the speaking area or a direct question to the audience.

Eye contact

"One of the most wonderful things in nature is a glance of the eye; it transcends speech; it is the bodily symbol of identity," said Ralph Waldo Emerson. And no matter how many words and how thoughtfully you deliver them, your audience wants to meet your eyes. It is not sufficient to look up from your notes or scan the back of the room. You must meet the gaze of individuals—they must feel your presence and your being and your energy. This is one of the reasons why practicing with an audience is crucial. You can't learn this skill in the mirror.

Response

Before you present your performance to your audience in practice, tell them what you hope to achieve (what we call an utterance): to say everything you wish to say to this audience in this context on this subject at this time to evoke a particular response. When you have finished, ask them to talk about their response(s). True, this is not the audience and context for which you prepared, but you will have some idea of whether or not your utterance is finalized. If they are puzzled, unconvinced, hostile to your ideas, or unmoved by your rhetoric, you may want to rethink, while you have the time.

Timing

Until you've mastered all the points up to here—adjusted your stance and breathing; improved your enunciation; practiced transitions, eye contact, and response with an audience—you're not prepared to make final timing adjustments. When you're pretty sure that your audience will be moving in the direction you desire, then you can do your final fine-tuning. And remember, there are not a lot of situations in which running over or under by a couple of minutes is of great consequence. If you are in one, use a timer each and every time you practice and get your speech down to the second. If you fear running over, make sure your crucial material is not at the end of your speech where it might get cut out, or make a plan to keep an eye on the time and leave out a specific section in order to jump to the end if time grows short.

BRAIN TICKLERS
Set # 36

Practice your speech with an audience to refine your use of transitions, eye contact, ability to elicit the response you desire, and timing. Write some notes about how practice changes your performance.

(Answers are on page 252.)

Reading

Reading performance may have some striking differences from what we've talked about so far, especially if you are reading a story. You may be seated, rather than standing, with one or two children on your lap, or you may be reading upside down as you hold a picture book on your lap so young children can see it while you're reading. Now that presents some challenges to the average reader! But in these situations, as elsewhere, practice helps, and many picture books are written with embedded rhythm and rhyme that will help make it easy for you to remember large portions of the text, if not the whole thing, easing your task.

In addition, the voice you use may *not* be your own—because a lot of the time when you read, it may be a better choice to be in character. Developing characters with the voice can be fun, but it is also challenging. The best model is storytellers or readers who convey a whole story themselves (no cast). Jim Dale is particularly adept at creating and keeping separate a wide variety of voices while narrating a story. Listening to his recordings, you can immediately tell which character is speaking. Here's another area in which working with an audience in practice will be extremely helpful in knowing how you're doing.

Gesticulation

Gesturing when reading aloud partly depends on what you are reading and partly on whether or not your hands are full of book. If they're not, your hands can help with characterization: you can keep one hand palm down on the book with your forefinger marking your place while you use the other hand, for example, to point, wave, offer, refuse, pat, slap, hit, signal okay, signal "thumbs up," or thumb your nose—whatever gesture would express the character's inner being at that moment.

Action

If you are reading an essay or other expository work, you may well deliver it in place. If, however, you are reading a story, and if you are not piled with children, you may use your freedom to change positions—you may go from sitting to standing; you may walk, stop, pause, and continue your stroll—whatever motion seems in keeping with the text and adds to your presentation. You can even, should the situation warrant, move among the audience.

Audience interaction

For many people, the first experience of being read to is couched within a conversation with an older person: the book has a place within a broader stream of communication. This creates for people the sense of being read to as an intimate activity—one in which the interaction is not formal and confined to the task at hand (one reads; the other listens) but is rather informal and can move from reading into discussion or commentary or questions or joint wondering about the book or about life. For other people, the experience of the story (see Poe's comments on page 144)—the suspension of disbelief and the sense of being in another place, another time, another world—is such an incredible gift that they do not want anything to break into or mar their experience. So you can have, in the same audience, the curious questioners and the eager shushers. For each performance, given the audience and the context, you must weigh the choices and decide if you want to offer the audience continuous interaction, or if you want questions saved for the end. Before you begin, you must make clear to the audience the parameters of the performance. If you are on a proscenium stage, you will have less of a problem encouraging your audience to hold their questions than if you are sitting cross-legged on the floor with them.

BRAIN TICKLERS
Set # 37

Practice reading with an audience to work on gesticulation, action, and audience interaction, as appropriate to your piece. Write some notes about how practice affected your performance decisions.

(Answers are on page 251.)

Speaking

If your speech focuses on a personal experience of high adventure, some of the advice for readers may well fit the bill for you. You may use vocal characterization and gesticulation to bring your story to life for your audience. If you are delivering a more formal speech genre, you are likely to adopt a less mobile voice and stance.

One occasion for a change of voice that you are likely to come across in a formal speech is a quotation. Sometimes a quotation is slipped seamlessly into place without any differentiation. But often it is introduced by a pause and a change of inflection to signal—without saying "and I quote" or "as —— once said" or something similar—that the material that is being said is from a source other than the speaker.

Preparing for audience response

Preparing for audience interaction should be a priority for a speaker. If the point of an utterance is to gain a response, then anticipating audience response is a key element of your preparation. Especially if you are trying to affect people's actions or values, if you can have the opportunity to find out how you did, why not take it?

As a speaker, you can take several different approaches to audience interaction. You can choose to interact directly with the audience from the moment you arrive. If you're speaking to your own class, this will naturally be the case, but if you're speaking to a group of people you don't know, you have a choice of making your speech more or less like a conversation. To foster interaction, you can

- ask the audience direct questions in the course of your speech,

- create opportunities for audience comments (invite them to raise a hand to indicate they have something to say),
- have the audience participate in demonstrations, quizzes, surveys, and the like (how many of you have ever . . . ?),
- allow time for questions and answers after your presentation is complete.

If you are going to allow questions, then prepare yourself for the most difficult questions you can imagine. Is there anything you left out of your speech? Be prepared to answer questions about it. Did you find any evidence that contradicted your thesis? Be ready to explain why you stuck to your ideas in the face of it. Other questions you should be ready to answer include:

- Who's your authority?
- Where did you read that?
- What do you mean?
- What's your evidence for that claim?

If you anticipate that you are likely to receive such questions, come to your speech prepared with the answers.

HELPFUL HINT

Any time you allow audience participation, you may receive questions that are irrelevant, inappropriate, or beyond the bounds of your subject or knowledge. Such questions should be dealt with calmly and evenly. You need to distinguish carefully between questions that are legitimate, though difficult or put to you by a person who is hostile to your point of view, and questions that are out of bounds, even if put by a well-meaning or friendly audience member.

BRAIN TICKLERS
Set # 38

Prepare for audience interaction during and/or after your speech, as appropriate for your situation. What questions do you anticipate? How will you answer them?

(Answers are on page 251.)

How much should I practice?

Whether you are reading aloud or speaking, professionals estimate that you will need four to six run-throughs. Remember that this is only an estimate. Length, complexity of material, or other factors may necessitate additional practice. The best rule is to practice until you feel as comfortable as you can feel in the situation (given time and other constraints). You should know your main points and ideas and feel comfortable expressing them. You'll probably have some phrases that you use every single time, and some that vary. Especially for your first experience, you want to feel that you've made the maximum effort beforehand to ensure success.

DELIVERING PREPARED MATERIAL

What's the difference between a dress rehearsal and the performance? Several things distinguish the two. Do you remember the discussion of performative language on pages 96–97? We treat language in rehearsal as ordinary and language in performance as performative. What we say in performance acquires a power and a meaning and an energy in performance *just because it's in performance* that it cannot attain in rehearsal, no matter how smoothly everything goes. Is it partly the anticipation? Or is it the sense of finality—that this is it? Or is it the coming together of all the elements—you, your audience, the occasion? Maybe it's all three.

Speech anxiety or stage fright

That sense of having only one chance can be glorious . . . or terrifying. Some people feel a bit (or very) overwhelmed by public speaking. Just being aware that you may become somewhat unsettled can help you maintain your poise. You should know that the energy that manifests itself in nervousness can be converted into positive vitality and enthusiasm that can energize your performance.

Identifying your concerns can help you address them in a positive way. If you are wary of speaking to strangers, you can do what many speakers do and take the time to greet and get to know a few members of your audience before your presentation begins. When you get up to begin, locate those people, and make a point of making eye contact with them. You'll have familiar faces to focus on as you talk.

If time constraints concern you, make sure that you arrive early. If you are sensitive to temperature, dress in layers and come early to assess the comfort of the room (keep in mind that rooms warm up as they fill with people). If you are concerned about your throat getting dry, bring a water bottle from which you can discreetly sip before you begin and after you finish. If you are speaking at a public function, you will usually find water provided on the speaker's platform. If not, you may feel comfortable asking for it.

Another thing you can do is decide beforehand whether or not you're the type of person who should do a last minute rehearsal or whether you should finish practicing the day before and give yourself a break. Based on your personality, make a decision about the kind of schedule that will help you have the most relaxed approach to your performance.

If you do feel nervous, here are some things that may happen and some actions you can take to help you cope.

COPING WITH SPEECH ANXIETY OR STAGE FRIGHT

Sign of nervousness	What you can do
choppy speech or too quick speech	Tap the toes of one foot inside your shoe in a moderate rhythm and read to the rhythm.
fidgeting hand motions	Depending on your situation: • Lightly rest your hands on the podium; • Hold your hands flat against your sides; • Put one palm down on your notes with your forefinger as an indicator to follow and the other on the edge of the stand.
giggling	Take several deep breaths and avoid making eye contact with a friend who might make you laugh harder.

What to do on the day of your speech

Whether you are performing a reading or giving a prepared speech, here are some guidelines for the day of your presentation.

Final copy of your notes

The final copy of your notes should be word processed or printed as large as reasonable to make them easy to read while making it possible not to have to turn pages. If you are placing them on a stand, you can probably count on two sheets resting side by side. Make sure you practice with your final copy at least once so that you know where on the page(s) things are.

What (NOT) to eat

Speech coaches advise that you avoid milk and dairy products prior to public speaking. Cabbage, carbonated beverages, and other foods that can cause burping and very spicy foods are also better skipped. It is also wise to avoid eating immediately before your performance. Plenty of water is advocated, and melon (like cantaloupe) and tart apples are recommended.

What to wear

If you are appearing in character or doing a demonstration, your outfit should reflect those requirements. Otherwise, your attire should reflect the formality of the occasion and your relationship with the audience. In any case, you should choose your clothes well in advance and wear them during practice to make sure that they work with any movements you have incorporated.

Where to stand or sit

The exact place to stand or sit may be predetermined and obvious when you reach the performance space. If you have a choice, you should judge by both sound and sight. Test the sound in the performance space, if you haven't had a chance to practice there. Begin saying your piece. You want to have the best sound and still be in everyone's line of sight. Consider the type of visual aide(s) you are using. Do you need to be near a spot on which to mount chart paper? Do you need a place against which to lean materials? Do you want to have an array of items in front of you that you can point to? Make your choices based on your particular presentation.

Timing

If you need to keep to a strict time, and you are unsure of the length of your presentation, ask a friend to sit in a visible spot in the audience and act as a timekeeper for you. At a preset warning time, your friend should discreetly raise his or her hand to signal you and then signal you again when your maximum time limit is reached. This will make it possible for you to focus on your speech and not on a stopwatch.

Watch your audience

Whether or not you have decided to allow your audience to speak during your presentation, you can allow them to give you feedback by watching their faces and body language. Are they smiling, thoughtful, perplexed, curious, engaged? Do you feel that they are "with you"? If you discover that your audience is different than you expected (in a really good mood, more sophisticated or thoughtful than you'd anticipated, already attuned to the issue about which you're speaking), you may want to change some of your remarks or to address the matter directly. For example, "I see by your reactions that many of you have more than a passing familiarity with the development of children's theatre in America, so I'm going to move on to some recent innovations in the use of multimedia in children's theatre."

Stand and deliver

There are two basic and very different ideas about public speaking. One is that the goal of public speaking is to say something original—that you may take the same old subject but use your creativity to put a new twist on the way it's perceived. The second idea is that everything's already been said but not by you. It's not what you say that matters anyway; it's how you say it. And because you are unique, you will say things in a unique manner.

I actually think both can be true. I would argue that even "I love you"—probably the most repeated phrase in human existence (if you count it in all languages)—is absolutely unique in every occurrence because the *I* and the *you* that exist in this moment have never existed before (and will never exist again), so the thought and the utterance are unrepeatable. I and you will both be changed by that utterance and be different from then on.

John Campbell wrote in *Speech Preparation* (1981, p. 41): "A speech is an incarnation, an idea in flesh—personality and personal contact are its very lifeblood." You used your mind when you thought about the ideas for your speech. Now you are going to use your body to convey those ideas to an audience. Whatever has happened in practice is one thing. Now is the utterance.

BRAIN TICKLERS
Set # 39

Are your final preparations complete for your performance? Create a checklist for yourself to help you next time you present. What do you need to do (and when) in order to make your preparation smooth and comfortable?

(Answers are on page 251.)

WINGING IT

If you have ever prepared for a reading or a speech, all that preparation wasn't just for that one event. No, all that work carries over, not only into the next reading or speech but also into all the unrehearsed reading and speaking you do.

Reading on the spot

Whether you're reading a story to a child you are baby-sitting, reading aloud a newspaper account of your brother's latest sports triumph to amuse your friends, or auditioning for a play, there you are with little or no time to prepare, trying not only to make sense of somebody else's words and guess where they're going but also maybe to create a character at the same time. That takes skill—and quick thinking! It can be especially challenging if you're reading with others (see pages 157–158) who aren't keeping up their end of things. If you're feeling frustrated, keep in mind that reading out loud is not a skill that has been widely taught. If your fellow readers are having difficulties, your best strategy (whether it is, in fact, the case or not) is to imagine that they are doing the best they can.

Auditions

Acting is a process of creating a character during which you internalize lines and action and portray the character in a more-or-less lifelike context within the given circumstances of the world—real or unreal—presented by the script. You are to give the illusion that what you are doing is happening for the first time every time you perform it.

At an audition, you (and perhaps some other actors) are usually in street clothes and may read prepared lines or lines you have never seen before (cold reading). The array of talent at an audition is just that—an array. Who knows whom you'll be reading with? So while an audition is the checkpoint you have to pass in many cases in order to act, what you have to be able to do in an audition requires some different skills than what you need to do as an actor.

Simply put, in a nonprofessional audition, these are the most important things in order:

1. How you enter the audition space (3 seconds);
2. How you walk to your spot where you will perform (10 seconds);
3. How you say your name (3 seconds);
4. If you *look* the part;
5. The material you perform (2 minutes most likely);
6. Your craft as an actor (plus any innate talent).

There are techniques for all of this, but the first 20 seconds are the most important, believe it or not.

If you are doing a prepared reading, it is generally a monologue—a speech for one character from some play, chosen to show the best you can do. The hints for reading aloud in Chapter 3, and for preparing in this chapter, as well as any acting instruction and coaching you have had will help you with your monologue.

Now, you may have to do a cold reading, a monologue or scene that you have never read before. You will have a few minutes to look at the scene. Here are some hints:

- Read through the whole scene. Think about your character. Ask yourself briefly about the Five W's surrounding your character's situation—Who, What, When, Where, and Why? Answer these questions (as far as you can): What are my character's age, ethnic background, profession, beliefs, interests, economic status? What is his or her life situation? Who are the significant people in his or her life?

- Read through once more. Think about the scene in terms of beginning, middle, and end. Answer these questions: What is the focus of the scene? What is my character's goal for this scene? What obstacles stand in the way? What is the central conflict? What happened just before this scene that precipitated this scene's action?
- Look for the key words. In each line, mark the word that should have the most stress. Mark pauses.

- Learn to "grab a line" and look up from the script to deliver it directly to your scene partner.
- When you do the reading, hold the book or papers in one hand. Follow the lines with the forefinger of your dominant hand.
- When your audition is complete, thank the director.

Reading texts in the classroom

Teachers sometimes cover material in class by having students read it aloud. This can give teachers the assurance that work has been covered, save homework time for students, and—for certain types of literature (e.g., scripts)—allow students to experience works in a manner that is closer to their originally intended purpose. It does, however, mean that students do some ice cold readings. Here are some hints on how to get the most out of this kind of experience.

- If you know you aren't good at ice cold readings and you're going to have to do them, practice. It doesn't have to be extremely painful. You can use your favorite magazine, and instead of reading one article silently, read it out loud. For practice in doing characters, read comic strips. Preface each character's lines by saying, "Then —— said."
- Think about your own learning. Reading aloud is primarily an aural experience. Are you an aural learner? If so, you're likely to benefit a lot from listening to your classmates. If not, here's a chance to strengthen a weaker area in your repertoire.
- If you're reading in a subject area, note the topic carefully. Look for key words (often boldfaced or printed in color) and stress them. Read at a moderate pace with distinct enunciation.
- If you're reading a script or a work of fiction, you can try to do some vocal characterization to make your part more meaningful. Remember that you can use all the flexibility and variation in the voice (volume, stress, pitch, tempo, tone, pauses, and timbre) to create character. If you're reading a script, look ahead for your character's next line and note the cue (the line before yours). If you're reading fiction, look carefully to see who's speaking before you begin to characterize the dialogue.
- If you're reading a poem, quickly identify the use of sound (like rhymes) and meter. See if you can identify the speaker. Use punctuation, not the end of lines, as stops.

Unrehearsed speaking

Unrehearsed speaking is a smaller version of a prepared speech. So you follow the same preparation steps, only more quickly, and you limit your subjects to those about which you can speak from your existing knowledge with little or no time for research and no rehearsal. Several different formats are followed. In one, you choose your own topic. In another, the audience proposes several topics, from which you may select one. The characteristic features are the sudden proposal to speak and the minimal preparation time. In any case, you can follow these steps:

1. Quickly assess the audience (page 173) and consider your favorite speech genres (page 179). Using those choices as guides, choose a subject (page 181) and purpose for your utterance.
2. Create a thesis statement (pages 195–196). Write it down.
3. Organize your talk by identifying tasks and major supporting points (page 199). Note them in outline form, leaving room above and below for your introduction and conclusion.
4. Brainstorm an introduction and conclusion. Note them briefly in your outline (see pages 210 and 211).
5. Choose a title (page 212). Write it at the top of your outline.
6. Stand up, gather your audience's attention, and deliver your speech. Robert F. Kennedy's speech (page 268) is an unrehearsed speech.

Answering questions in class

You may have a whole new perspective on answering questions in class if you think of the questions (when appropriate) as mini-tasks using the task analysis on page 191 and compose your answers accordingly. If you are a visual learner, you may even picture one of the graphic organizers in your mind's eye and run through it as you speak.

Oral examinations

Many people have never experienced an oral examination. For those who feel challenged taking written examinations and are more comfortable speaking, oral examinations can be a welcome change. You just demonstrate your knowledge in a different mode.

Here are some hints for doing well in an oral examination:

- Write out a list of questions that you think you may be asked and practice with a friend. For each question, identify the answer with a task type/relationship/graphic organizer (see page 191), and use that structure to organize your answer. Think about creating a finalized utterance for each answer.

At the exam:

- If you don't receive questions in advance, listen carefully to each question and focus only on it. You may repeat it, if that helps you to be sure that you have understood. If you are unclear about what is required of you, ask for clarification before you begin your answer.
- Unlike a written examination, where you are graded only on what is on your paper, in an oral examination, your attitude, posture, attire, level of formality, eye contact, and poise all contribute to the impression you create because they are part of your communication.
- If you do not know an answer, state so plainly. If you have something pertinent to add, such as how you would find it out (I know that to solve this problem I need to apply the formula for projectile motion, but I have forgotten it), do so briefly.
- Unlike a written examination, in which the questions are set before you arrive, the questions in an oral examination are often formulated based on your performance. The examiner will question you to test the limits of your knowledge. Therefore, unlike a written examination, on which you may achieve a perfect score, you are likely to receive questions that you are unable to answer in an oral examination. If you have mastered the material you were supposed to cover, do not consider this a failure; it is not like leaving a blank on a written exam, and it does not mean that you will not do well.

Improvisation

Improvisation is unscripted theatre that usually engages from a set of *given circumstances*, a term that comes from Stanislavski. Although actors create dialogue and actions spontaneously as they perform—with the result that improv worlds tend to transform quickly sometimes—the requirement of dramatic unity remains constant. Improvisation requires shared assumptions. Each actor and the audience agree to accept the other actors' imaginations as real for the sake of the fun to be had by all.

Improv is a valued learning tool, used for many years by teachers in the classroom and by directors in rehearsal. **Spot improv**, a more recent development, uses suggestions from an audience to prompt the creation of short, entertaining scenes. There are many, well-tested improv systems and improv-based theatre games available in books and on the Internet.

Improv Games:

http://www.learnimprov.com/
http://www.lowrent.net/super/improv/games.html
http://www.humanpingpongball.com/

Meetings

Meetings often combine prepared presentations with impromptu question-and-answer sessions. You can treat this type of meeting much like an oral examination, and remember that a speech is a speech is a speech—you can prepare using the same guidelines for a meeting as for other speaking opportunities.

Job interviews

Job interviews are also like oral examinations, but they are nearly always formal and are usually characterized by a highly predictable set of questions for which you can prepare yourself. Here are some of the standard questions that you may expect to be asked, depending on your age and experience. To gain comfort, have a friend ask you the questions, and answer them as carefully as you can. Ask for feedback, and revise your answers. As in oral examinations, treat each question as a minitask. Frame it for yourself in a structure, and make sure that your utterance is finalized.

- Tell me about yourself. (Best answer: What would you like to know?)
- What type of position are you interested in? or What is your ideal job?
- What led you to decide to seek a position with this company?
- What salary do you want to make in this job?
- Where do you see yourself five years from now?
- If you are hired, how long do you plan to stay with this company?
- How do you explain gaps in your work history? low grades? terminations? a lay-off?
- What is your greatest weakness?
- What is your greatest asset or strength?
- What do you bring to this company that we will not find in any other candidate?
- In what context have you given your best? How could we help you give your best if you worked for this company?
- How do you handle stress?
- How do you deal with difficult people?
- Tell me about a time when you received criticism for your work or an idea.
- What have you done that shows initiative?
- How do you approach working in groups? Do you tend to play a particular role?
- Describe the positive and the negative aspects of your previous job.
- Why do you think you would enjoy this kind of work?
- What do I not know about you that would help me make my decision?
- Do you have any questions?

Always thank the interviewer before you leave. You should have an expectation of when you might hear back from the company about whether you have gotten the job or the next round of interviews.

EVALUATING SPEECH

It is likely that many of your presentations will receive informal or formal evaluation—anything from the audience's applause to a letter grade from a teacher or professor. But it's a good idea for you to evaluate your own performance, regardless of how others perceive it. You can use any rating system that suits you such as 1–5 stars, letter grades, or + or −.

EVALUATION FORM FOR PERFORMANCE

Criteria	Rating	Notes for next time
End result		
Achieved finalized utterance • communication said all you wanted to say in the place and time on the given subject and was appropriate to context and audience and was answerable		
Audience responded as desired • act • feel • think • commit to, value		
Composition		
Introduction caught attention		
Body supported thesis • accurate • complete • specific • authoritative • relevant • logical		

Criteria	Rating	Notes for next time
Body organization served well • good transitions • identifiable tasks		
Conclusion ended effectively		
Language use		
Appropriate speech genre • unified presentation		
Delivery		
Vocal expression • enunciation • rate • flow • stress • pauses • characterization		
Bodily action		
Gesticulation		
Eye contact		
Paralanguage (facial expression, etc.)		
Appropriate use of visual aide(s) and equipment		
Poise		
Audience interaction handled gracefully		

There is a proverb that says, "Words are the only things that last forever." If they're going to last so long, we may as well send them out into the air bearing valuable, true, funny, vibrant, vital thoughts. What do you say?

BRAIN TICKLERS—THE ANSWERS

Set # 34, page 223

Answers will vary. **Possible response:** Yes.

Set # 35, page 227

Answers will vary. **Possible response:** Because I tend to slur my words, putting *a* between each word helped my speaking.

Set # 36 through Set # 39

Answers will vary.

Appendices

APPENDIX A—GRAPHIC ORGANIZERS

These graphic organizers are models for you to adapt to your purposes. Modify them as necessary to suit your particular needs by adding, subtracting, or changing elements.

Comparative Analysis—Compare/Contrast (Type 1 or Type 2)

Venn Diagram

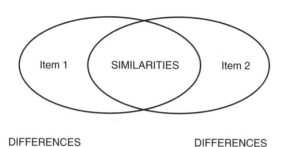

Item 1   SIMILARITIES   Item 2

DIFFERENCES   DIFFERENCES

Item 1   Item 2

SIMILARITIES

DIFFERENCES

Operational—Define (Type 1) or Sequence (Type 2)

Process

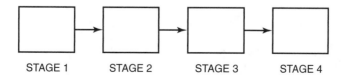

STAGE 1   STAGE 2   STAGE 3   STAGE 4

Operational—Define (Type 2) or Sequence (Type 2)

Flow Chart (modify as necessary to fit operational analysis)

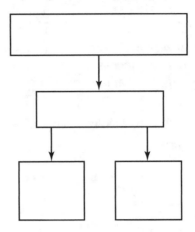

Structural—Define (Type 3)

Concept

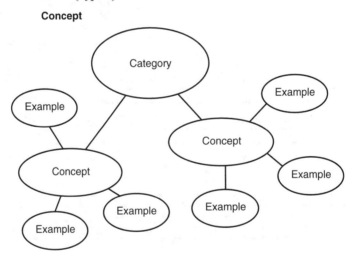

Sensory—Define (Type 4)

Spider

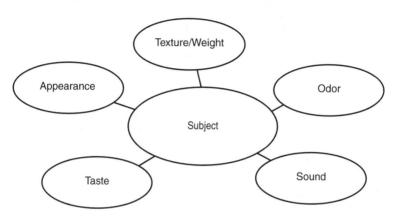

Relational—Define (Type 5)

Interaction (modify as necessary to fit relational analysis)

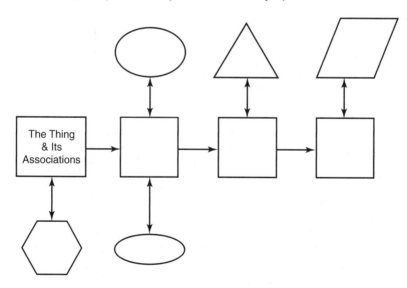

Theoretical/Meaning/Thematic—Define (Type 6)

Proposition/Support

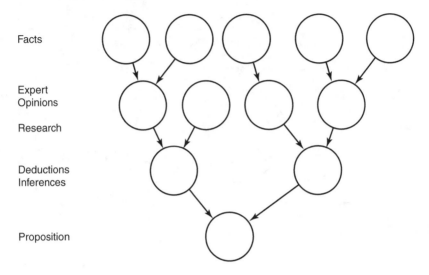

Facts

Expert
Opinions

Research

Deductions
Inferences

Proposition

Utilization—Define (Type 7)

Results

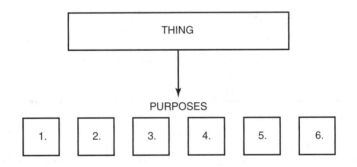

Evaluative—Define (Type 8)

Criteria and Rating

CRITERIA	RATING
1.	
2.	
3.	
4.	
SUMMARY	

Situational—Define (Type 9)

Modified Spider

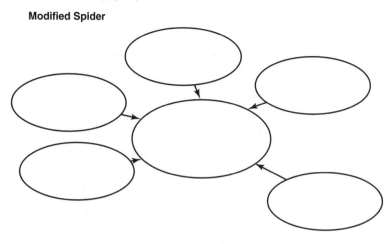

Logical—Argue (Type 1; Type 3)

Hypothesis (see also Proposition/Support)

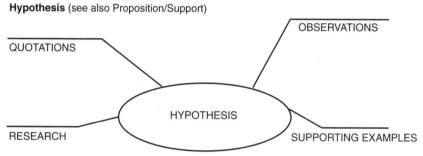

Problem/Solution—Argue (Type 2)

Problem/Solution

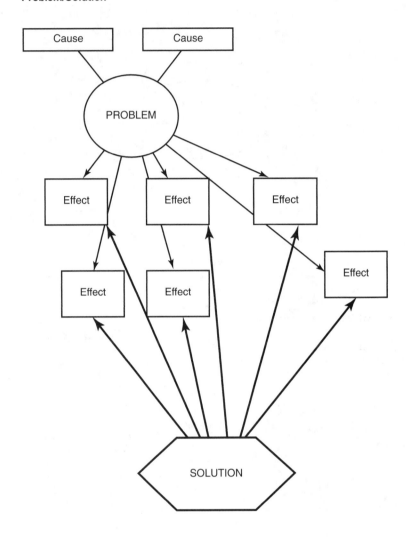

Question and Answer—Argue (Type 4)

Question/Answer

Question: _____

_____

Answer: _____

_____

↑

Supporting Details:

1.

2.

3.

Cause/Effect; Response; Emotional—Sequence (Type 1)

Fishbone

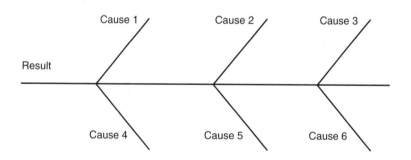

Cause/Effect with levels

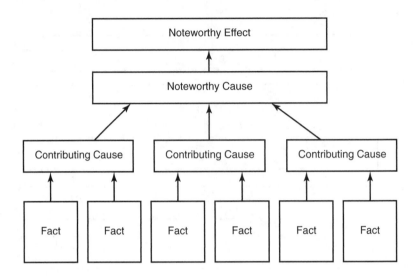

Historical—Sequence (Type 2)

Timeline

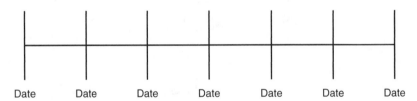

Classification—Classify (Type 1)

Subordination (indicate position of the thing you are classifying, for example, with *)

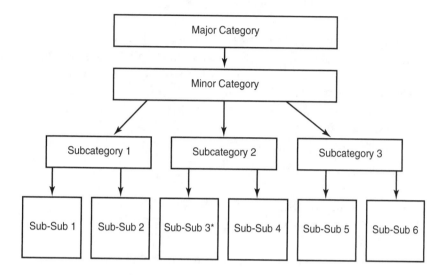

APPENDIX B—SELECTED SPEECHES

Here are some great speeches from American history that you may wish to read and study. Following, is a list of web sites that have text and/or audio or video versions of famous speeches. Listening to or watching famous speeches after becoming familiar with the text is an especially valuable tool to hone your public speaking skills.

Ain't I A Woman?

Sojourner Truth (1797—1883) delivered this address to the Women's Convention in Akron, Ohio, in 1851.

Well, children, where there is so much racket there must be something out of kilter. I think that 'twixt the negroes of the South and the women at the North, all talking about rights, the white men will be in a fix pretty soon. But what's all this here talking about?

That man over there says that women need to be helped into carriages, and lifted over ditches, and to have the best place everywhere. Nobody ever helps me into carriages, or over mud-puddles, or gives me any best place! And ain't I a woman? Look at me! Look at my arm! I have ploughed and planted, and gathered into barns, and no man could head me! And ain't I a woman? I could work as much and eat as much as a man— when I could get it—and bear the lash as well! And ain't I a woman? I have borne thirteen children, and seen most all sold off to slavery, and when I cried out with my mother's grief, none but Jesus heard me! And ain't I a woman?

Then they talk about this thing in the head; what's this they call it? [Member of audience whispers, "intellect."] That's it, honey. What's that got to do with women's rights or negroes' rights? If my cup won't hold but a pint, and yours holds a quart, wouldn't you be mean not to let me have my little half measure full?

Then that little man in black there, he says women can't have as much rights as men, 'cause Christ wasn't a woman! Where did your Christ come from? Where did your Christ come from? From God and a woman! Man had nothing to do with Him.

If the first woman God ever made was strong enough to turn the world upside down all alone, these women together ought to be able to turn it back, and get it right side up again! And now they is asking to do it, the men better let them.

Obliged to you for hearing me, and now old Sojourner ain't got nothing more to say.

The Gettysburg Address

On November 19, 1863, President Abraham Lincoln dedicated the Union cemetery at Gettysburg with this speech.

Four score and seven years ago our fathers brought forth on this continent a new nation, conceived in liberty and dedicated to the proposition that all men are created equal.

Now we are engaged in a great civil war, testing whether that nation or any nation so conceived and so dedicated can long endure. We are met on a great battlefield of that war. We have come to dedicate a portion of that field as a final resting-place for those who here gave their lives that that nation might live. It is altogether fitting and proper that we should do this.

But in a larger sense, we cannot dedicate, we cannot consecrate, we cannot hallow this ground. The brave men, living and dead, who struggled here have consecrated it far above our poor power to add or detract.

The world will little note nor long remember what we say here, but it can never forget what they did here. It is for us the living rather to be dedicated here to the unfinished work which they who fought here have thus far so nobly advanced. It is rather for us to be here dedicated to the great task remaining before us—that from these honored dead we take increased devotion to that cause for which they gave the last full measure of devotion—that we here highly resolve that these dead shall not have died in vain, that this nation under God shall have a new birth of freedom, and that government of the people, by the people, for the people shall not perish from the earth.

I Will Fight No More Forever

Chief Joseph of the Nez Perce (1840?–1904), known as "Thunder Traveling to the Loftier Mountain Heights," led the resistance against the takeover of Nez Perce lands by white settlers in Oregon. Ordered to move to a reservation in Idaho in 1877, Chief Joseph agreed at first, but after members of his tribe fought several battles with the U.S. Army as they tried to flee to Canada, Chief Joseph surrendered with this speech on October 5, 1877.

Tell General Howard I know his heart. What he told me before, I have it in my heart. I am tired of fighting. Our Chiefs are killed; Looking Glass is dead, Ta Hool Hool Shute is dead. The old men are all dead. It is the young men who say yes or no. He who led on the young men is dead. It is cold, and we have no blankets; the little children are freezing to death. My people, some of them, have run away to the hills, and have no blankets, no food. No one knows where they are—perhaps freezing to death. I want to have time to look for my children, and see how many of them I can find. Maybe I shall find them among the dead. Hear me, my Chiefs! I am tired; my heart is sick and sad. From where the sun now stands I will fight no more forever.

William Faulkner's Nobel Prize Acceptance Speech

Upon accepting the Nobel Prize in literature in Stockholm, Sweden, on December 10, 1950, American Novelist William Faulkner presented this address.

I feel that this award was not made to me as a man, but to my work—a life's work in the agony and sweat of the human spirit, not for glory and least of all for profit, but to create out of the materials of the human spirit something which did not exist before. So this award is only mine in trust. It will not be difficult to find a dedication for the money part of it commensurate with the purpose and significance of its origin. But I would like to do the same with the acclaim too, by using this moment as a pinnacle from which I might be listened to by the young men and women already dedicated to the same anguish and travail, among whom is already that one who will some day stand where I am standing.

Our tragedy today is a general and universal physical fear so long sustained by now that we can even bear it. There are no longer problems of the spirit. There is only one question: When will I be blown up? Because of this, the young man or woman writing today has forgotten the problems of the human heart in conflict with itself which alone can make good writing because only that is worth writing about, worth the agony and the sweat.

He must learn them again. He must teach himself that the basest of all things is to be afraid: and, teaching himself that, forget it forever, leaving no room in his workshop for anything but the old verities and truths of the heart, the universal truths lacking which any story is ephemeral and doomed—love and honor and pity and pride and compassion and sacrifice. Until he does so, he labors under a curse. He writes not of love but of lust, of defeats in which nobody loses anything of value, of victories without hope and, worst of all, without pity or compassion. His griefs grieve on no universal bones, leaving no scars. He writes not of the heart but of the glands.

Until he learns these things, he will write as though he stood among and watched the end of man. I decline to accept the end of man. It is easy enough to say that man is immortal simply because he will endure: that when the last ding-dong of doom has clanged and faded from the last worthless rock hanging tideless in the last red and dying evening, that even then there will still be one more sound: that of his inexhaustible voice, still talking. I refuse to accept this. I believe that man will not merely endure: he will prevail. He is immortal, not because he alone among creatures has an inexhaustible voice, but because he has a soul, a spirit capable of compassion and sacrifice and endurance. The poet's, the writer's, duty is to write about these things. It is his privilege to help man endure by lifting his heart, by reminding him of the courage and honor and hope and pride and compassion and pity and sacrifice which have been the glory of his past. The poet's voice need not merely be the record of man, it can be one of the props, the pillars to help him endure and prevail.

Robert F. Kennedy Eulogizes Dr. Martin Luther King, Jr.

At a political rally supporting his campaign for the Democratic presidential nomination on April 4, 1968, Robert F. Kennedy realized that the crowd was unaware that Dr. Martin Luther King, Jr. had been assassinated and made this impromptu announcement.

Do they know about Martin Luther King? [speaking to a rally organizer]

Man in crowd: No. We've left that up to you.

Kennedy: Could you lower those signs, please? [People lower their "RFK for President" picket-signs.]

I have bad news for you, for all of our fellow citizens, and people who love peace all over the world, and that is that Martin Luther King was shot and killed tonight.

Martin Luther King dedicated his life to love and to justice for his fellow human beings, and he died because of that effort.

In this difficult day, in this difficult time for the United States, it is perhaps well to ask what kind of a nation we are and what direction we want to move in. For those of you who are black—considering the evidence there evidently is, that there were white people who were responsible—you can be filled with bitterness, with hatred, and a desire for revenge. We can move in that direction as a country, in great polarization—black people amongst black, white people amongst white, filled with hatred toward one another.

Or we can make an effort, as Martin Luther King did, to understand and to comprehend, and to replace that violence, that stain of blood shed that has spread across our land, with an effort to understand with compassion and love.

For those of you who are black and are tempted to be filled with hatred and distrust at the injustice of such an act, against all white people, I can only say that I feel in my own heart that same kind of feeling. I had a member of my family killed, but he was killed by a white man. But we have to make an effort in the United States, we have to make an effort to understand, to go beyond these rather difficult times.

My favorite poet was Aeschylus. He wrote: "In our sleep, pain which cannot forget falls drop by drop upon the heart until, in our own despair, against our will, comes wisdom through the awful grace of God."

What we need in the United States is not division; what we need in the United States is not hatred; what we need in the United States is not violence or lawlessness; but love and wisdom, and compassion toward one another, and a feeling of justice toward those who still suffer within our country, whether they be white or they be black.

So I shall ask you tonight to return home, to say a prayer for the family of Martin Luther King, that's true, but more importantly, to say a prayer for our own country, which all of us love—a prayer for understanding and that compassion of which I spoke.

We can do well in this country. We will have difficult times; we've had difficult times in the past; we will have difficult times in the future. It is not the end of violence; it is not the end of lawlessness; it is not the end of disorder.

But the vast majority of white people and the vast majority of black people in this country want to live together, want to improve the quality of our life, and want justice for all human beings who abide in our land.

Let us dedicate ourselves to what the Greeks wrote so many years ago: to tame the savageness of man and make gentle the life of this world.

Let us dedicate ourselves to that, and say a prayer for our country and for our people.

Tribute to the *Challenger* Astronauts

On January 28, 1986, the Space Shuttle Challenger *exploded shortly after takeoff from Cape Kennedy, killing all seven astronauts aboard, including New Hampshire teacher Christa McAuliffe. President Ronald Reagan addressed the nation, quoting from this poem:*

HIGH FLIGHT

*Oh, I have slipped the surly bonds of earth
And danced the skies on laughter-silvered wings;
Sunward I've climbed, and joined the tumbling mirth
Of sun-split clouds and done a hundred things
You have not dreamed of wheeled and soared and swung
High in the sunlit silence. Hov'ring there,
I've chased the shouting wind along, and flung
My eager craft through footless halls of air.
Up, up the long, delirious, burning blue
I've topped the windswept heights with easy grace
Where never lark, or even eagle flew
And, while with silent, lifting mind I've trod
The high untrespassed sanctity of space,
Put out my hand, and touched the face of God.*
—John Gillespie Magee, Jr. (killed in the Battle of Britain, age 19)

Ladies and gentlemen:

I'd planned to speak to you tonight to report on the state of the Union, but the events of earlier today have led me to change those plans. Today is a day for mourning and remembering. Nancy and I are pained to the core by the tragedy of the shuttle *Challenger*. We know we share this pain with all of the people of our country. This is truly a national loss.

Nineteen years ago, almost to the day, we lost three astronauts in a terrible accident on the ground. But we've never lost an astronaut in flight; we've never had a tragedy like this. And perhaps we've forgotten the courage it took for the crew of the shuttle. But they, the *Challenger* Seven, were aware of the dangers, but overcame them and did their jobs brilliantly. We mourn seven heroes: Michael Smith, Dick Scobee, Judith Resnik, Ronald McNair, Ellison Onizuka, Gregory Jarvis, and Christa McAuliffe. We mourn their loss as a nation together. For the families of the seven, we cannot bear, as you do, the full impact of this tragedy. But we feel the loss, and we're thinking about you so very much. Your loved ones were daring and brave, and they had that special grace, that special spirit that says, "Give me a challenge, and I'll meet it with joy." They had a hunger to explore the universe and discover its truths. They wished to serve, and they did. They served all of us.

We've grown used to wonders in this century. It's hard to dazzle us. But for 25 years the United States space program has been doing just that. We've grown used to the idea of space, and perhaps we forget that we've only just begun. We're still pioneers. They, the members of the *Challenger* crew, were pioneers.

And I want to say something to the schoolchildren of America who were watching the live coverage of the shuttle's takeoff. I know it is hard to understand, but sometimes painful things like this happen. It's all part of the process of exploration and dis- covery. It's all part of taking a chance and expanding man's horizons. The future doesn't belong to the fainthearted; it be- longs to the brave. The *Challenger* crew was pulling us into the future, and we'll continue to follow them.

I've always had great faith in and respect for our space pro- gram, and what happened today does nothing to diminish it. We don't hide our space program. We don't keep secrets and cover things up. We do it all up front and in public. That's the way freedom is, and we wouldn't change it for a minute. We'll continue our quest in space. There will be more shuttle flights and more shuttle crews and, yes, more volunteers, more civil- ians, more teachers in space. Nothing ends here; our hopes and our journeys continue. I want to add that I wish I could talk to every man and woman who works for NASA or who worked on this mission and tell them: Your dedication and professional- ism have moved and impressed us for decades. And we know of your anguish. We share it.

There's a coincidence today. On this day 390 years ago, the great explorer Sir Francis Drake died aboard ship off the coast of Panama. In his lifetime, the great frontiers were the oceans, and an historian later said, "He lived by the sea, died on it, and was buried in it." Well, today we can say of the *Challenger* crew: Their dedication was, like Drake's, complete.

The crew of the space shuttle *Challenger* honored us by the manner in which they lived their lives. We will never forget them, nor the last time we saw them, this morning, as they prepared for their journey and waved goodbye, and "slipped the surly bonds of earth" to "touch the face of God."

Great speeches sites

http://www.pbs.org/greatspeeches/timeline/index.html
http://www.historyplace.com/speeches/previous.htm

Speech and Transcript Center

http://gwu.edu/%7Egprice/speechhistoric.htm

Inaugural Addresses of the Presidents of the United States

http://www.bartleby.com/124/

Online Speech Bank

http://www.americanrhetoric.com/speechbank.htm

APPENDIX C—MARKED TEXT

The three selections in Appendix C contain answers for Brain
Ticklers 19, 20, and 21. Each demonstrates a way of marking a
text for reading aloud. Because there is not a definitive way to
mark text, you will not find a complete answer here. The sports
essay and story each have two paragraphs marked. The scene
from a play is the script belonging to the actress playing the part
of Hannah and shows her score with her notes.

Dress for demonstrating exercises.   *Visual aides: Slides=ᴧᴧᴧ*   *underline=stress / = Breath or Pause*

Golf Fitness: What You Don't Know Might Hurt You

by Dr. John J. Bisaccia,
Certified Sports Chiropractic Physician

For years golf was considered a game played by non-athletes
and older individuals. / It seemed to lack the essentials of
competition, / i.e., / fit athletes demonstrating skill and
endurance / while competing head-to-head in exciting matches
for large sums of money. / However, / with the arrival of
players such as Tiger Woods and David Duval, the face of golf
and the idea of a golfer as a non-athlete have changed
drastically. / As if by some revelation, / professional golfers
came to realize that being physically and aerobically fit could
lead to longer drives, / more powerful iron shots, / and greater
endurance, / while all along decreasing their chance of a
career-ending injury. / These ideas have reached recreational
golfers, / who have now started to work out in hopes of
turning bogies into birdies. / While the potential for improving
their game is enormous, / it must be done with sports-specific
principles as opposed to generic workout routines. /

273

The PGA recognizes physical fitness as one of the six basic aspects to the game of golf, to be given equal weight with ³ equipment, basic instruction, advanced instruction, mental preparation, and course management. With that in mind, more and more amateur golfers are now taking advantage of sport-specific training towards golf in order to improve their own games and ward off or improve on injured areas. Injuries for amateur and professional golfers are very common. However, the two groups of golfers tend to have different areas that become injured. A right-handed professional will most likely suffer from left wrist pain, lower back pain, and left shoulder pain, in that order, while a right-handed amateur golfer will most likely suffer from lower back pain, left elbow pain, and left shoulder pain, in that order. In fact, lower back injuries to amateur golfers constitute 53% of the injuries treated. So regardless of the level of play, the lower back appears to be the vulnerable site for injury.

Injuries to the lower back may be caused by a combination of factors, including faulty swing mechanics, poor flexibility, inadequate trunk strength, and overuse. The golf swing requires the spine to rotate, bend laterally, and extend, three motions that do not combine naturally. During a single round of golf, a player may swing the club between 200 and 300 times on average, including practice swings. Multiply that times rounds per year and driving range practice, and you can see why this repetitive action can lead to injury of the discs, muscles, and facet joints of the spine. In fact, research has demonstrated that amateur players generate greater stress on the lower back than professionals. The reasoning is that less than optimal swing mechanics equates to more damaging motions. "What we lack in quality we make up in quantity." Thus correct posture and proper conditioning plays a major role in the prevention of lower back injuries.

In analyzing many golfers' physical capabilities, some general conclusions can be drawn. Most male golfers suffer from inflexibility, especially of the hamstrings, hip flexors, and lower back muscles, while most women golfers suffer from lack of strength in the glutes, abdominals, and oblique regions. Although these two combinations are different in the realm of treatment and conditioning, both these physical weaknesses lend toward injury in the lower back region. In addressing the inflexibility component, stretches for the hamstrings, hip flexors, and mid to low back regions are as follows:

In addressing the strength of the glutes, abdominal, and oblique regions, the following exercises could be very helpful:

Lunges

Crunches

Bicycle kicks

Russian twist

Balance on one foot

Bench press/push ups

Flexibility of the hamstrings, spinal muscles, and hip flexors can be accomplished by the following:

Knee to chest

Double knee to chest

Rotational stretch

Hip flexor lunge

Hamstring

For stretching, hold each stretch for 30 seconds, 2 repetitions, 1 time a day. Do not bounce—hold a steady tension and remember to breathe.

For strength exercises, perform as many repetitions as possible till fatigued.

For balance exercises, maintain position for up to 2 minutes.

One aspect to note is that although a female golfer may not benefit as much from performing the stretching exercises, most male golfers would benefit from adding the strengthening exercises as well. If you have a lower back or other health problem that prohibits you from doing these exercises, please talk to a trained sports-specific professional to help you customize a program to fit your needs. Both men and women would benefit from at least 30 minutes of cardiovascular exercise (walking, biking, Stairmaster, etc.) four times a week to build endurance and heart health. This is very important, especially for a golfer who walks the course and finds himself/herself fatigued towards the 14th and 15th holes, barely having enough stamina to finish the 18th. Take a look at your scorecards and see how your performance declines as the golf day progresses.

Golf is a wonderful game that we can play throughout our life, especially into our elder years. Proper strength and conditioning can not only help you play better in the present moment, but can secure a future for you in this sport.

"An analogy is when 2 things are alike. The story I'm going to read to you has an analogy in it. See if you can figure out what 2 things are alike. The story is called:"

NELL'S KITTENS   AN ANALOGY

by A.D. Laberge

ʌ by

ll for pause
= for stress

This big, old house has been a stagecoach inn. The house is nested into a steep hill. So steep is the hill that the *contrast* back door is on level ground and the front door is very, very high up. Perhaps once there was a high porch. Now the old *contrast* inn is mainly empty, except for Jon and Nell the cat. They are good friends. Nell often curls up on Jon's lap hoping to get *pause here* rubbed behind the ears or gently stroked. Nell is a country cat—small, gray, friendly, and clever.

DO YOU KNOW A NICE CAT?

Nell feeds herself. She's a very good hunter. Country cats eat mice, moles, birds, and any little creature they can catch. A cat's skill as a mouse catcher is very valuable, especially on a farm. Often Nell brings her supper home and surprises Jon. Jon // being a person and not a cat // sometimes is squeamish when he finds Nell's supper on the rug by their bed. But he understands that Nell is behaving just as a cat should. *("That means that seeing Nell's dinner makes his tummy feel funny.")*

WOULD YOU EAT DINNER ON A RUG?

Jon notices that Nell's slender sides seem wider. For 63 days she grows wider and wider. Until one morning Jon hears sounds from his big, cardboard, laundry box. He looks into the box, and there is Nell with 3 tiny babies, as small or smaller than your hand. One is white, one is spotted, and the littlest is gray, just like Nell. The kittens can't walk—they mostly sleep. Their eyes are closed, and their ears are folded back. They can't hear or see yet.

HAVE YOU EVER TRIED TO SLEEP IN A CARDBOARD BOX?

Nell suckles her kittens until they are full of milk. Eating and sleeping helps them to grow. Jon leaves nutritious food and fresh water for Nell, near the big brown box. After 3 days, Nell leaves for a short time to hunt for her own food. As the kittens grow, Nell's trips away from the laundry box get longer.

Nell is a patient mother. Her kittens are busy growing and learning. Their eyes open after 12 days. They learn to use their legs just like children do. First they crawl, then they walk, and then they run. By the time the kittens are 35 days old, they are little scampering, stumbling balls of fluff. The kittens have learned to eat and drink and run and play. Jon loves to watch this silly stumbling circus of kittens. But soon the tiny acrobats huddle together and sleep—growing and playing takes lots of energy.

DO YOU THINK YOU GROW WHEN YOU SLEEP?

Nell knows a mother is a teacher. She speaks to her kittens with greeting, scolding, and warning sounds. She teaches by example. One day she brings back a very lifeless mouse. The kittens play & bat the small, gray morsel around, thinking it's a toy, not knowing that Nell is starting to teach them how to hunt.

DO YOU PLAY WITH YOUR FOOD?

As the kittens grow, Nell increases the challenge—each time the mouse is more and more lively. The final mouse is quick and healthy. Nell drops the mouse on the rug. It runs. The kittens run. The mouse is very fast—it runs away. The kittens are learning. They learn the smell of a mouse, the sound of a mouse, the quickness of a mouse, and the taste of mouse.

HOW COME CAT FOOD ISN'T LABELED "MOUSE" FLAVOR?

Next Nell brings her kittens outside, to the yard in front of the big, old house. Her tail is a flag they can follow. They play hide-go-seek, follow-the-leader, and stalking games in the tall grass. Play is the work of children and kittens—they learn as they play. Nell's kittens have a lot to learn before they can catch their own food and take care of themselves.

WOULD YOU LIKE TO BE A COUNTRY KITTEN?

An example of how an actor might score a script   *(CHANNAH'S SCRIPT)*

A cutting taken from the play THE NEW SURVIVORS,* Scene Two: *Terezin—We Must Survive!* (pp. 13-17)

HANNAH   "GRAB" THE FIRST LINE AND PLAY THESE ACTIONS FROM THE READING POSITION.

(Lifting her head. Spots Darren.) Darren, wake up! Go stand guard! Tell us if anyone is coming.

PLAYING A GAME AT NIGHT UNDER EXTREME DANGER WILL MAKE THE SITUATION MORE EXCITING, MORE THRILLING

STRESS THIS AS A LOUD STAGE WHISPER.

(Darren gets up and looks out the side window.)

DARREN

No guards! I'll tell you if I see any.   I CAN GIVE DARREN A THUMBS UP HERE.

HANNAH   PANTOMIME SHAKING EMILY & SARA WITH ONE HAND

Emily, Sara, let's wake the others. JUST GESTURING

* "GRAB" ALL LINES

EMILY

(Still mostly asleep, she responds too loudly.) WHAT?

IF READING IN A CIRCLE - GRAB + MAKE EYE CONTACT WHEN APPROPRIATE
IF IN A LINE FACING AN AUDIENCE - GRAB + PRETEND TO MAKE EYE CONTACT BY PLAYING ALL LINES FORWARD

* Shell-scripting is a theatrical technique that allows me to use my craft as a professional theatre artist/educator to blend a successful and aesthetic script from the work of community or school participants (who may be actors or non-actors, but who are not theatre professionals) who come together to collaborate in creating social issue theatre specific to an existing community or school problem. *The New Survivors* is an excerpt from the result of a shell-scripting process in an elementary school fifth grade classroom confronting issues of violence after 9/11: They chose to address the issue by working with me to create a theatre piece exploring the Holocaust

Van Johnson

HANNAH

Shhh! You want to get us all killed?!!

→ SUBTEXT: "I FEEL RESPONSIBLE." ↙ WITH A GESTURE
LOOK BRIEFLY AT DARREN. ASK HIM TO GIVE A GESTURE THAT MEANS— "IT'S STILL OK".

EMILY

Sorry!

SARA

(Still mostly asleep and grabbing Emily's foot by mistake.) Hannah is that you?

TRYING TO SURPRESS MY OWN LAUGHTER AS I ENJOY MY TWO CLOSE FRIENDS

EMILY

(Retrieving her foot.) Sara, it's me, Emily! OK? And this is my FOOT, not Hannah

SARA

Sorry, Em - mil - lee! (To Hannah.) Are we going to play the Animal Game?

EYE + BODY EXPRESSIONS

HANNAH

Yes! Wake the others.

FLASH HER A LOOK.

AD LIB HERE.

(The three girls hurriedly wake everyone to play the Animal Game.)

EMILY

(Too loud.) HANNAH, CAN I GO FIRST!

INTERNAL DIALOGUE
"WHAT HAVE I DONE? WE'LL ALL GET CAUGHT."

HANNAH

WAVING AN ARM AT EMILY TO QUIET DOWN. I MIGHT LOOK AT DARREN TO GET THE OK TO CONTINUE

Shhhhh! Yes, but we've got to be quiet.

OVER ARTICULATE WITH LIPS

EMILY

Ok, I was alive in this millennium, but I'm extinct! (Emily begins her pantomime: the extinct Great Auk.)

INTERNAL DIALOGUE
"THAT'S A GOOD ONE EMILY
I CAN'T HELP
ESPECIALLY ME, BUT SMILING"

PAVEL

That's easy, you're a duck!

(Laughter followed by lots of *shhhhh – ing!*)

EMILY

Ducks are still with us today, dah!

INTERNAL DIALOGUE
"I WOULDN'T HAVE KNOWN THAT ONE."

RUBIN

Oh, I know. You're a Great Auk.

EMILY

Yes. (To Pavel.) See, Pavel!

HANNAH

INTENTION: TO KEEP THE GAME MOVING
AND TO AVOID CONFLICT. "I AM RESPONSIBLE:
INTERNAL DIALOGUE."

Ok. You win a turn Rubin.

RUBIN.

USE TO TAKE CONTROL. TAKE FOCUS.

OK, I'm alive millions of years ago. (Rubin pantomimes being a Brontosaurus eating treetops.)

EMILY

You're a dinosaur!

PAVEL

Yes, but what kind?

EVA

A Tyrannosaurus Rex. (She pantomimes goofy viciousness.)

AD LIB GESTURES THAT
INDICATE I'M STILL KEEPING
TRYING TO KEEP
CONTROL AND QUIET. YET I
EVERYONE CANNOT HELP SMILING

(Controlled laughter at Eva's goofy response.)

PAVEL

No.

(But, Eva continues her goofy performance until she gets the laugh she wants.) AD LIBS CONTINUE

RUTH

(Ruth has had enough.) Eva, it's eating the tops of trees. It must be a Brontosaurus.

PAVEL

Yes. Ruth's turn.

DARREN

(Shouting in a big whisper.) Gestapo!

(They all return to a sleeping position.) BUT, I AM THE MOST ALERT IN PRETENDING TO SLEEP. I STAY READY

They're passing by us. They went into another barracks. All clear. INTERNAL DIALOGUE: —"IT'S NOT YOUR TURN, ALEX." I GIVE HIM A DISAPPROVING LOOK.

ALEX

Hey, what am I? (He pantomimes being a Tyrannosaurus Rex.)

RUTH

(Still wanting a turn.) Rubin just did that one Alex. You're a Tyrannosaurus Rex.

ALEX

Wrong. I'm an EVA! (He jumps at Eva with a roar and begins to tickle her. Eva screams as others begin to tickle her also.)

I IMMEDIATELY BEGIN GESTURING TO QUIET THE FUN. I'M NOW WORRIED.

DARREN

GESTAPO! (All freeze.) They're headed for the train.

(All the children gather and look out over the audience.)

DAVID

Look! It's those poor children from Poland. Must be over a thousand of them.

I VISUALIZE THE SCENE AS I STARE FORWARD, NOT MOVING, MY BODY RIGID. MY INTERNAL DIALOGUE: "THIS WILL BE US ONE DAY SOON."

ALENA

They were part of that uprising against the Nazis in their Polish ghetto.

NINA

They've only been here a couple weeks. *TEARS FILL MY EYES*

285

ALENA

All trains heading that way go to Auschwitz from here (MY EYES SHUT.)

NINA

Gas chamber.

ALL

(Quietly with felt meaning.) Gas chamber.

[Handwritten annotations:]

MY FACE DISTORTS INTO A FULL, GENUINE SILENT SOB. I REPEAT THIS THOUGHT OVER+OVER IN MY MIND—"WE MUST SURVIVE! WE MUST SURVIVE!" MY BOTTOM LIP STRENGTHENS.

HOLD UNTIL LIGHTS FADE TO BLACK.

MY EYES OPEN JUST BEFORE I SPEAK

GLOSSARY

ad lib (from *ad libitum*—in accordance with desire) to improvise lines or actions

gesture a movement that reveals the character's intention, spontaneous reaction, or specific communication; in theatre, all gesture must have meaning

give and take focus to purposely stop the flow of action and refocus attention; bring focus to one's self or pass it on

grab a line when reading dialogue from a script, read ahead to get the line in your head so that you can look up (interact realistically) to deliver it

intention what the character intends to do in one *beat*; each beat is a unit of action which taken all together make up the character's *super-objective* (the character's main objective that motivates a character throughout the entire play); thus intentions and beats are not separate and fragmented but only useful, working subdivisions of what is, and must appear as, a coherent whole (since dramatic unity requires that everything must interrelate)

internal dialogue when we are just shy of one year old as children, we begin a conversation with ourself inside our brain that cannot be stopped until we die or experience brain trauma

pantomime to convey with body and facial movements and no words

play all lines forward deliver lines facing the audience, not to the other actors

scoring a script preparing a script for a production by marking all of the important information that is needed on it; a script may be scored by an individual actor, by the director, or by the stage manager, each score reflecting the material for which that person is responsible

stage whisper a loud whisper that is meant to be audible to the audience but within the world of the play is accepted as having the carry of a normal whisper

subtext what the character is really feeling or thinking beneath the spoken text and action of a play

INDEX